SPLIT-LEVEL ELDERS

By Paul E. Stine

Cover designed by Austin Stine

Table of Contents

Chapter 1: Polyester Thieves

I've had it with this road. Two hundred traffic lights and every single one is red. Red, Red, RED! It's no wonder we put makeup on in the car, otherwise, we'd fall asleep.

The brakes on my Honda are taking the brunt of my exasperation as I head to Mom and Dad's – again. Second time this week – an emergency run to the grocery store for bananas. That's all she'll buy, some damn bananas and maybe an onion.

Oh, and a half gallon of milk, if the expiration date suits her. She's very flexible on those expiration dates. On one trip she'll say, "No, Sissy, it expires in a week. We won't use it by then." The next time it's, "I'll take it. It doesn't expire for a week. We go through the milk."

Well, Mom, which one is it?

She doesn't know, but I do – it's whichever irritates me the most. That's how she makes decisions. No, wait – it's not the store today, it's the doctor. That's even worse.

I'm daydreaming – or nightmare-ing, if that's a word – on my way to Stan and Gladys Ray's split-level ranch. An hour drive to reach the ornery octogenarians. That's what my husband, Theo, calls them, among other things. He's a brainiac without a single answer to any of my questions about Mom and Dad, like, "Why do I do this? What manner of guilt must I possess? Why don't I tell them to hire a cab, or a house cleaner, or a mower? Why don't I tell them to order a pizza?"

Oh, that's right – I have told them these things, but they won't do it. Period.

And it's not because they don't have the money. That's the really infuriating part. They can afford to get some help, but they don't want help, they want Sissy Woodson. They don't want — there goes my darn cell phone.

"Hey, Sissy," she starts, "I didn't think you were going to answer, it rang so long."

My God, it's my sister. If I'd known it was her, I might not have. Her voice is gravelly, like she just woke up.

"Hi, Brenda. I'm in the car. My phone was in this beach bag I call a purse. How are you?"

"I tried your house. Where you heading?"

"Mom and Dad's"

"Oh." She sounds disappointed.

"Why? What's wrong?" I know something's wrong – she wouldn't call me otherwise.

"My damn car wouldn't start. I was going to see if I could bum a ride. Guess you're a long way?"

"Yeah. I'm on Sixty-eight stuck in this boulevard of red lights." But the good news is – it's safe to talk.

"I don't guess Theo's around?"

She must be desperate – she hasn't spoken with him in a year. I glance at my watch. "I'm sorry. He left for school early today."

I'm watching the truck in front of me. The left signal's been on for half-a-mile. Whoever it is, they really plan ahead.

"Oh. Well, how are Mom and Dad?"

The tone of her voice is obligatory. If she really wanted to know, she'd call or come by once in a blue moon. "Great. Turns out Mom's a blast and Dad's Mr. Cheerful."

She laughs, low and gruff. "Sure. I'll bet."

"They're fine. Mom's shoulder is bothering her. She's got an appointment at ten-thirty."

"They called me about a week ago, but I was so busy."

I already know that. Dad said, "We couldn't reach your sister. Something must be wrong with her phone."

It's unbelievable the excuses they invent for my only sibling. She's six years younger than me, which makes her fifty-two going on fifteen. She's a self-centered serial divorcee big as a cow but less useful. Car problems – that means we'll see her for the first time in three months.

She doesn't wait for me to respond. "Uh, well, how are the boys?"

It sounds like she's stalling. She probably wants to find out if one of them can come and get her. "Everybody's good. T2 is in New York this week, I think, and Brian's at school."

Theo Jr., our oldest, owns a consulting business. I think it's fair to say he's loaded. Brian is twenty-seven, and he just finished his doctorate. He's teaching, working for his father, Theodore Woodson, Sr.

"Gosh, I haven't seen you guys for so long. Mom says you're skinny as a rail. Must be nice to be tall and thin?"

"I'd rather be rich." And the *thin* part is debatable. I'm five-eleven and a hundred-fifty pounds and I have been for twenty-five years. "I have to stay in fighting shape to do battle with her, and Dad's a pain in the ass too. Anything new with you?"

"She said your hair was short. Did you get it cut?"

"Yeah – couple of months ago. It's been so hot. Charlie put some streaks in it. Covered up the gray. What's happening in your life?"

There's a short pause, then, "Oh, hey," she says, "I got another call. It's probably my ride. I better go. Tell everybody I said Hi."

What ride? "Okay. Good luck." I set my phone in the cup holder next to my liquid assistant, Mr. Chardonnay.

I don't drink alcohol excessively, just excessively early. I need something before I deal with Stanley and Gladys. I have Xanax, but I'm worried about becoming addicted. Sometimes I worry so much I have to take a Xanax. Over the last four years I've become an expert on cheap wines. I've even devised what I call the Sissy Substitution Formula: One-half bottle of wine equals one Xanax. Don't try looking that up in one of those *How to Cope with Difficult Elders* books, it's my own invention.

The time between 8 and 9 am is Pinot Noir Hour. I cheated a little this morning. I took one whole pill with one glass of wine. As I walked out the door, I decided that might not be enough, so I poured another glass into a Styrofoam cup. I already know where the dumpster is behind the old middle school. I'll get rid of the evidence there.

I'm taking Mom to her drug supplier. She can barely move her right arm because her bursitis is so bad. That's to be expected. Wednesday she used a toothbrush to "scratch out that dirty area where the carpet meets the baseboard. Dirt just piles up there."

As I pull into their narrow drive, I steel myself. The door opens before I reach it because she's been waiting for me. We exchange a hug. At eighty-seven, she's shrunken and wispy.

"Oh, come in," she says in her fragile voice. She's dressed, but she has her housecoat on overtop. She shuffles into their small kitchen. "Stanley's on his walk. That dumb walk of his," she barely gets out.

She means the walk that Dad's done every day since his heart attack twenty-six years ago. The walk that probably keeps him alive. I don't say anything because one of the books on dealing with these people says not to confront them about things *unless it could harm them*.

"How you feeling? Shoulder any better?"

"Oh no," she laments, "I can hardly move it at all. It's just right through here," and she rubs it. "I don't know why it's started hurting again. My knees hurt too."

I'm shocked. Shocked! You mean crawling around on the floor to disinfect the carpet/baseboard interface might not be the cause? But, again, I don't bring it up. I tried doing that for years, and it doesn't work.

My new tactic is to refuse to issue *should* statements. As I recall that includes *should not* statements as in, you should not crawl around on your knees to clean the carpet/baseboard interface.

"Maybe she can give you something," I tell her in my most sympathetic tone. I set my purse on the counter, bend down and give her a kiss on the forehead.

"I don't know." Her whine barely manages to escape her thin lips before trailing away.

I lack the vocabulary to adequately describe my mom's voice. It's a cross between a plaintive cry from a dying animal and a violin played by an infant. It's moaning mumbles about the loss of God and terrible bunions. It's consistently baleful. It fits her perfectly.

She leans against the beige Formica countertop, back hunched over, slightly concave. Her paunch completes an S shaped body capped by loosely twisted gray-brown hair. She's the picture of misery. She has migraines every couple of weeks, but she refuses to take the medicine because her share of the cost came to fourteen dollars a month. That's right – fourteen dollars – as in a ten and four ones.

"Did you take one of your pain pills?"

She cringes. I must have hit a sore spot.

"I ran out. Maybe she'll give me some more today."

"I thought you had a month's worth."

She babbles something I can't understand.

"What?" I ask.

"No," she says as she wipes her nose with the ever-present tissue.

"I'm sure it was. Where's the bottle?"

"No, no, that won't help now."

"Why not?"

"Well," she breathes sorrowfully, "it just won't."

Now I'm suspicious. Her shoulder hurts, and she won't show me the bottle. Surely she hasn't taken them already? "The doctor won't write another one till it's out."

She hobbles over to the dull stainless-steel sink shaking her head and mumbling "No." Then she looks up at me. "They didn't work that well anyway."

"Anyway what?"

"Brenda's head was hurting her," she finally admits.

"So, Brenda took them?"

"Well, not all of them," she says defensively, "just the ones I wasn't using."

I want to ask her which ones she wasn't using, but she'll just say it was the ones she gave Brenda. I'm trying to remember what the books said about this? Oh, that's right, NOTHING! They didn't mention this possibility. I need the book with a chapter that says, *How to handle your difficult older parent who supplies drugs to your sibling addict*.

And Brenda's been here sometime in the last few weeks. Mom didn't mention that, probably because she gave her the pills. I could absolutely explode.

But I don't. Instead, I tell myself to calm down. Every time I tell myself to calm down I hear Theo's voice. "Now calm down, Sissy. Just calm down." His voice is deep, like it started in his toes and traveled six-and-a-half feet losing all the high notes on the way. With gray-blond hair and a craggy face, he reminds me of a Swede on steroids.

"Okay," I say, resigned, "just tell McWerther. I'm sure she'll understand."

"Well," she snivels into her tissue.

This will be our last trip to this office because Dr. McWerther's returning to hospital work. Her replacement isn't due for a couple months. Unbeknownst to Mom and Dad, I'm planning a change to a doctor who makes house calls at Beeler's Trace, a retirement community. It's fifteen minutes from my house, and that's where I intend for them to reside in the near future. I'm sick of this drive.

"You ready?" I ask.

Loading her into my car is a ballet of errors. First, she stumbles out of the house wearing that housecoat, which appears to have been stolen from a VA ward circa 1920.

"Mom, your housecoat?"

"Oh." She looks down at herself.

I help get it off and then follow her very detailed instructions on where it should be placed "in my bedroom closet next to my winter housecoat, but not the green one with the stripes – the other green one. It's heavier – on the left. Use the hanger with the paper cover, or it could get rust on it. Watch that door, it gets stuck. Don't push Stanley's shirt up against anything because it bends the collar, and he doesn't like that, and he'll want me to wash it again . . ."

Now she creeps around the car to my side.

"Are you going to drive?"

"Oh!" and she laughs like it's the funniest mistake ever made. "I'm getting as bad as your father."

She walks around the back of the car because that's the longest route. When she arrives she says the same thing she always does, "I can do it, Sissy." I have to wait until she concludes that she can't do it, because, "Your car is so hard to get into."

Our Goldilocks car collection includes a BMW (too low), Theo's Escalade (too high), and my Honda. I haven't learned what bars her from getting into the Honda yet. Is there such a thing as "too average"?

Once I get her in, tuck her wrinkled XXL blouse under her worn, shiny, burgundy polyester pants made into Capri's by placing the waistband just below the breasts, it's time to wrestle her seatbelt into place. I'm not sure when Mom would have needed a blouse this big, but since she's shrunk to the size of a ten-year-old with growth issues, the blouse covers the whole center console including the seatbelt receptacle.

"Careful. Careful." she says as I try to find the latch. And now she'll tell me about Dad pinching her leg with the buckle and how he should have been more careful. "Watch out," she admonishes when I close the door.

In the car, she goes back to focusing on that mystery of her shoulder and knee pain.

I try to change the subject. "Don't you have anything nicer to wear? What about those new outfits I got for you a month ago? What you're wearing is way too big."

She's busy fighting her billowing blouse against the air conditioning vents. I reach across the console, capture the fluttering bubble and stuff it under her seatbelt.

"They make you wear a gown."

I nod as I back out of their drive.

"You have to take off your clothes," she continues.

"So?"

"You put them on that hook behind the door."

"Yeah?"

"Then they move you to another room for pressure checks."

"Pressure checks?"

"Blood pressure, Sissy," she says in her withering voice, like I'm an idiot.

"Okay."

"They're just hanging there," she finishes, as though that explains everything.

"So what, Mom?"

She looks at me, mouth slightly twisted. "Anybody could take them."

"Take your clothes?" I ask with astonishment.

"A patient," she says. "A patient might. Or maybe a nurse or a doctor."

"Mom, nobody wants your clothes. Why on earth would somebody want to steal your clothes?

That's ridiculous." Then I remember how I'm supposed to handle this: *get rid of the problem by lowering the level of conflict.*

"Maybe you're right," I tell her. "I suppose people might want your clothes. Polyester is making a comeback."

"That's silly," she says. "They don't want these old things. I swear, Sissy, sometimes I worry about you."

Me too, Mom. Me too.

"But the new ones," she continues, "they'd take those."

"Especially those thieving doctors," I say.

"They just want your money." Her cross-hatched face takes on a satisfied smirk since I'm in apparent agreement with her preposterous position.

She talks bad about "Stanley," all the way to the office where I wrestle her out of the car and into the waiting room. I sign her in, then sit beside her. I already know the answer to my next question, but I ask anyway.

"Do you want me to go in with you?"

Her hands are wringing away like she's trying to remove something wet and sticky.

"Well?" I ask.

"Of course not," she whispers. "A visit with the doctor is a private matter, Sissy. You know that."

At least it is for her, and it would be for anyone who planned to go in and tell a bunch of lies. The waiting room is already full. I hope they're not behind.

"Okay," I say. "That's fine."

I spend the next twenty minutes looking through *Golf Digest,* since I'm such a big golfer. I pay no attention to Mom's disparaging comments about everyone who gets called back: "She's too heavy . . . He shouldn't be by himself . . . She looks mean . . . He's too young to need a doctor . . . I hope that's not his wife . . ."

My mother makes Moliere's Alceste look like a piker. Her misanthropy is only exceeded by her skillful lying, usually by omission.

Last year she quit taking her thyroid medicine; it made her constipated. She pretended she didn't know what was wrong, and McWerther doubled the dosage. That's when I got involved. I met with McWerther and explained what I was dealing with. Now, we have a system.

A woman in faded scrubs appears at the door. "Gladys Ray?" she calls. I help Mom get up, and she follows the woman down the hall. Ten minutes later the woman motions to me. "Mrs. Woodson," she says, and I follow her until she pushes a door open to an examination room. "She'll be right in." I thank her as she pulls it shut.

It takes a few minutes before Dr. McWerther knocks, steps in and butts the door closed.

"Hi, Sissy," she says, and she's holding a thick folder. She gives me a sad, worn smile.

"Hi. Thanks for seeing me."

"No problem." She points to a chair as she sits down. She rests the file on her tiny lap, flips through a few pages and brushes a strand of straggly brown hair out of her face.

"I can tell your mom's in pain." She looks up at me. "Said she was out of Lortabs."

"You remember my sister, Brenda?"

"Yeah. Heavyset woman?"

I nod. "She got some of them. I don't know how many."

I feel comfortable telling her the truth, even though it's embarrassing. Maybe that's why I like her.

She closes the file. "Told me she doubled up. Said they didn't work."

"Hard to tell what the truth is with her," and I shrug. "If you'll give her some more, I'll keep them – dole them out."

She sets the file on the counter, and then runs one hand through her flat, thin hair. Her frock is too long, and then I notice it says *Dr. Hatcher* on the pocket in script. It's early, but I think she's already had a bad day. These old people have beaten her down. Maybe that's why she's going back to the hospital.

"Still having the migraines?" she asks.

"That's what she says. She won't take the Migranol. Says it makes her constipated, but it's the cost, really."

She shakes her head in resignation. I'm guessing she hears that a lot from this group.

She nods as I continue. "They won't do anything if it costs. It's like an illness. Dad's the same way."

"Well," and she stands, "You may have to, you know, take over eventually. I'm going to write a prescription for Vicodin. It's a little more powerful. One month. I strongly advise you to hold onto them. They're addictive, and I'm not talking about your mom."

Her hands barely peek out of rolled cuffs as they search for pockets. She looks down as if to see what the problem is. "This thing," she says.

I nod as I stand up. "Thanks. Yeah, it's kind of big."

"It's Hatcher's. He left a year ago. I don't know what happened to mine. Someone must have stolen it."

Well, I'll be damned. I laugh. "Maybe it'll turn up. I'm sorry you're leaving."

"I'll still be around, just, well," and she hesitates, "no insurance to deal with. It's getting worse and worse. If she needs to see somebody, before Dr. Lane gets here, ask for Dr. Sims. Sorry we're so busy today."

"To tell you the truth, I'm trying to get her and Dad hooked up with that doctors' group that makes house calls at Beeler's, but they don't know it yet. We're trying to get them to move over there."

She nods, bending to write on her pad. "Well, good luck. I hope they get better results."

"Not likely," I say. "They'll fight me if I try to take over. I'm hoping it doesn't come to that."

She smiles sadly and shakes my hand. "I'll give this to her." She holds up the prescription.

"Thanks."

I hustle back out to my chair, but it's taken. If Mom finds me sitting somewhere else, she'll be suspicious. I hear her voice, so I walk outside the entrance, count to ten and then head back in.

"There you are," she says in her accusatory voice. "Where were you?"

I wait until we're away from the office. "I had a call. Theo just wondered when I was getting back."

"Well, that's nosy," she huffs.

I turn on her. She moves away, fear on her old, weathered face. It's bad enough that they call five times a day, but I'm not listening to any crap about Theo.

"Give me that," I demand, and I take the prescription out of her hand and pretend to read it. "You'll get these seven at a time. You should be ashamed, giving your pills to Brenda. You know better."

"She had a head--"

"Be quiet!" I bark as I open the car door. "Now let's go."

She was silent nearly all the way home, but I knew it wouldn't last. "Your dad and I are worried about you."

"You should be," I tell her. "You should be worried that I get this filled and take the whole damn bottle. That's what you should be worried about."

"Sissy!"

"Don't 'Sissy' me." I try to calm down. "You live too far away."

I navigate the drive-thru at Walgreens, take Mom back to the house, get her inside, count out seven pills and put the bottle in my purse. Dad is taking his nap so I don't have to fool with him.

She thanks me all the way out and offers to pay five dollars for my gas. I should tell her to shove it, but I don't. But I don't take it either. I just look at her and shake my head. She wants me to take that money so she'll feel better.

"My name's Sissy," I say to myself, as I go through the door, "not Brenda."

I tried my deep breathing exercise on the way home, but the only real help was Theo, Xanax, and Lindeman Chardonnay, Bin 65.

Chapter 2: Real Estate Realities

As predicted, Brenda is insinuating herself back into our lives. She's even agreed to take Mom and Dad to see their attorney to make the annual changes to their will.

But then Brenda develops one of her situational migraines. They appear any time she's supposed to go over there. They're also synchronized with the holidays.

Dad called three times begging me to take them to their appointment before I finally relented.

"What is that all about?" asked Theo.

"I don't know," I told him. "Every year it's the same. But I'm going to find out."

Instead, I get here and Mom's still in her house robe and her hair's a mess. And she's got a damn migraine.

I follow them back to the sunroom addition, which I call the hothouse. I'm not sure what the temperature is in here, but I'm about to suffocate. "What's the air set on?" I nearly scream. I'm so mad she didn't call me and cancel.

"Oh," says Mom. "Your dad says it's not working right." Her head moves around like a chicken pecking the air.

"It's not," Dad says forcefully. You can always tell when he feels right about something – he speaks up. And he only feels right when he agrees with her. He's unshaven, and I can tell that we're not going anywhere.

I walk over to the thermostat.

"My God, Dad," I say in frustration. "It's on eighty-two." I turn it down to seventy-five. "Come on in the dining room," I shout.

"Now you know your mom doesn't want to use up the good furniture," he says slowly and carefully while looking at her.

Dad reminds me of Mr. McGoo, the way his heavy black-rimmed glasses slide down his scarred nose. His age spots have expanded to cover his whole face. If his clothes were any older, he'd be in a toga.

I pull out a seat at the far end of the thirty-year-old Duncan Phyfe dining room table that hasn't been used for thirty years. The seats are still covered with plastic, as they have been since they were new. Atop the plastic is a square piece of felt-backed tablecloth cut to fit each seat – Mom's idea of extra protection.

They still haven't moved from the hothouse, so I whip out my cell phone to call Theo. I don't really need to talk to him, but as soon as I start whispering so Mom can't hear me, she'll come running. And like the lackey he's become, Stanley will follow.

Dad's like an old dog loping along behind his mistress, waiting for an order, hoping not to offend. At eighty-seven, he's bent, but not from age. It's the stoop that comes from extended cowering to a power without logic or direction.

I decide at the last minute not to dial Theo, mainly because it'll just piss him off to find out I had to drive all the way out here for nothing. Also, it's embarrassing. So I pretend to call. I say

"Hello," loudly. I turn away, bend my head down toward my lap and mumble. "They really screwed me this time," I say so low that even I can barely hear it. "Yeah, screwed me good. What? Okay. Yeah. I've got it. Right."

By now I can hear them starting to move. Mom slithers in while Dad gropes along behind her.

"I got to go," I say loudly.

I can tell that Dad's embarrassed. He's got his hands stuffed down into his corduroy trousers and his head has nearly disappeared below the zip-up collar of his ancient sweater vest. It's the hottest summer on record, the house is an oven and Dad's dressed like a Fifty-fourth Street bum missing his stolen grocery cart.

They stand at the far end of the dining room. They don't want to sit down at the table, a style wholly at odds with the rest of their vintage 1975 neo-modern furniture. Mom seems to topple forward a bit, placing her hands on the glass-covered tabletop. Dad scurries around to pull a chair out, helps her sit, then sits down.

And now it's up to me. It's as though I'm sitting at a table with two special-needs children who've done something they know was bad, but don't know why. I love my mom and dad, I mean, aren't we supposed to? But they're driving me up a wall, and I can't walk away like Brenda. I feel obligated. It's payback time for being well-raised. I keep telling myself that they're old. But when I look at them sitting at the end of this table, my anger boils up.

"You knew we weren't going. I can't believe you didn't call."

Mom twists in her seat. "Well, Sissy, I thought I'd feel better by the time you got here. But I don't. So that's that. You can't tell . . ." and her voice trails off into the ether. Then she seems to come alive again. "Brenda has them too. You're so lucky you don't have them. Poor Brenda. She gets them just like me."

Poor Brenda my ass. Poor Brenda didn't spend an hour driving over here. It's times like this when I don't know what to do. I remember Theo saying, "Sissy, you've got to face it – they're not going to change."

If he's right, why beat them up? What's the point? On the other hand, they shouldn't get away with it. Won't that encourage more of it?

"I'm going to tell both of you something right now; I'm very angry that you let me drive all the way out here. If you just wanted to see me, then you should have asked me to come. But you should have told me the truth."

"Now, Sissy," says Mom, forcefully. "I told you the truth. I thought I might feel better by the time you got here. What else can I say?"

Both of them are squirming around, looking at a room they never use.

"Did you take your medicine?"

"It gives me constipation," and she looks away.

"They make different kinds. Every damn pill gives you constipation except pain pills. I'd rather have constipation than a migraine, but you won't even try something different."

I don't know why I bother; it's the same conversation, over and over again. Dad's head keeps getting closer to the placemat. He doesn't want any part of this.

"Well?" I say.

"Some of them cost a lot," says Mom.

That's a bunch of bull, and this isn't about money. It's about martyrdom. She wants me to understand that she's foregoing needed medicine to save a few bucks. She's suffering so that Brenda and I will have a grand inheritance. They want me to legitimize their incredible frugality. They want me to bow down in homage to their continuing sacrifices, all on our behalf. They want me to celebrate their pain and suffering. Celebrate their misery, justify their discomfort, all for me and Brenda.

They have vastly underestimated the irritation of two-hundred traffic lights this morning. And they've overestimated the importance of their money. I leave in a rage.

At home, Theo and I talk about it, and I decide that I've had enough. He calls our realtor, Dickey Jimenez, to set up an appointment at their house. They are going to move to Beeler's, or I'm done. I've had it.

#

It took seven days to agree on a real estate rendezvous:

Day One – rational discussion: "That house is too much work," I say, and "Beeler's is a wonderful place," and "Let's just get a price idea."

Day Two – pleading my case: "It's so long a drive," and "You'll be closer to the stores," and "They have shuttle service," and "It doesn't mean you have to sell."

Day Three – Increasing frustration: "I've explained everything ten times," and "You better sell while the market's good."

Day Four – Scare tactics: "Dad's going to croak mowing that yard in a hundred degrees," and "You won't need that damn ladder at Beeler's Place," and "I can't get to your place more than once every two weeks."

Day Five – Ultimatum day: "You agree, or you can find another daughter," and "Just pay somebody to drive you," and "I don't want to talk about it anymore."

Day Six – I refuse to take their calls.

Day Seven – A late-night message from Dad that they'll think about it.

#

Theo was going with me to Mom and Dad's, but he had to cancel at the last minute. He's caught at work, which is unusual, some kind of meeting with a Regent and a prospective donor. So I'm off to meet Dickey Jimenez, an old friend of ours. Dickey has handled our real estate moves a couple of times, and he worked for T2 when he and his wife, Alicia, bought the big house in Devonwood. We feel obligated to use Dickey, but we've warned him about Stan and Gladys Ray. I think he believes we're overreacting to their peculiarities. I called him right after Theo called to give him one more chance to back out, but he was insistent. He even offered to go alone, but that's like knowingly sending a child to face a pair of dragons; I just can't do it.

As I near their house, I see him getting out of his real estate car in their driveway. It's a Lexus of some kind, standard issue for agents. He moves to the front of his car and raises a camera. He tilts his head back, and I notice the bald spot in his white hair that gives him a monkish look.

I pull in behind him as he takes a picture. "There's a sign of some misplaced optimism," I say to myself.

"Hi, Sissy," he says as I get out. "Did Theo leave you stranded with this job?"

I laugh. "I guess so."

He gives me a hug. "My goodness," he says, "are you sure you're not Theo's daughter? You get taller every time I see you."

"It's these shoes. My jeans are too long."

"How are T2 and Alicia?"

"They're good. They love the house."

"Well, who wouldn't," he says, and he clips the camera to his belt while turning back to face the house.

We both stand there a few moments looking at it until I say, "You know, we've warned you about these two."

"I'm sure it'll be fine. It's a split-level," he says as he follows me, "so that's not real good;

they're not that popular anymore. But it should be okay in this neighborhood."

"I'll say this," I tell him, "it's clean. Mom's a cleaning fanatic."

He nods as we climb the three concrete steps up to the small square porch. The door magically opens. They've been watching from the living room. That's the only time it's used.

I introduce Dickey as we stand in the foyer. Mom is mumbling and backing away as if Dickey had a communicable disease.

"The yard looks nice," says Dickey.

"I do it," brags Dad. "Can't find anyone else these days."

That's true, especially if you don't look.

"Well," says Dickey, "if you'll give me a short tour we can sit down and talk about it." He looks around. "I like this foyer. Most splits around here don't have a foyer, even a small one."

Mom slinks toward the kitchen. I wonder if she's going to hide somewhere. Dad conducts the tour. I follow along behind them, waiting for the lies that are sure to come.

"Very nice," says Dickey as he follows Dad into the small living room, its perfectly preserved furniture arranged in stark symmetry. Two wall plaques of minstrel players adorn the wall above the faux fireplace. I remember them from when I was young; Dad got the holes wrong, Mom threw a fit, and he had to paint the wall again.

"It's more than two-thousand square feet," says Dad in his first lie of the day. I'm sure it's smaller than that.

"I'll get some measurements," says Dickey as he follows Dad into the dining room.

"I'll meet you back here," I tell them. I've decided to locate Mom to see if I can get her to join us. She's standing in the hothouse addition looking out back toward the neighbors. I can see the man who lives behind them walking to his back door.

"That's Jim," says Mom. "I wonder what he's doing home on Tuesday. I wonder if he's been fired."

"I guess that's possible, or he could be off today. Why don't you come to the dining room and hear what Dickey has to say?"

"We could sit out here," she says.

"It'd be better if we could sit at a table so he can get his stuff out." I'm treading as delicately as possible.

"What stuff?"

"You know – paperwork. You might have to sign something."

This seems to startle her. "Oh!" she says, "we're not going to do that today. You're always trying to rush us."

"Okay, okay. But at least be polite and listen."

Dickey and Dad are standing at the top of the stairs looking down at us. Dad's telling him how nice the small addition is. "Okay," I hear Dickey say, "Why don't we look at what I've brought?" They head to the dining room.

"He wants to give it away," Mom says quietly. "Don't think I don't know what's going on. But if he says it, I know you've got to do it."

She's talking about Theo. He's making them do it. No – that's not right. He's making me make them do it. Fine. Any time they don't like something I do, they blame it on Theo. He is in total control of my brain.

"Maybe you could offer him a Coke or something," I say.

She grunts. "He's the one getting paid."

I'm not sure if "he" is Theo or Dickey.

"Well," I say calmly, "they're in the dining room. I hope you'll join us." I head up the short flight of steps to the front level.

Dickey is getting some papers out of his briefcase. "Hi, Sissy," he says as I enter. "Is your mom coming?"

I look at Dad. "I don't know." I sit down.

"Now Gladys, you come on in here," says Dad. I hear Mom grunt, but she limps up the steps and sneaks past the doorframe.

"Can I get you something?" she asks.

"No, thank you, Mrs. Ray," says Dickey.

Mom pulls out a chair and uses the table to lower herself into it.

Dickey smiles and shuffles through the papers. "As I was telling your husband, I pulled some comparable sales this morning from houses in this neighborhood. It's close to Crandle Elementary, so that's a plus. Now, if you'll take a look at these," and he hands them several pages, "you can see that I've circled the price per square foot in red. Two of these are split-level ranches like yours. The other two aren't, but they're still a good indication of prices around here."

Mom looks at the papers and pushes them
away. I retrieve them.

"So," he continues, "these four houses, and
three of them are on your street, sold for an average
of $127 per square foot. The lowest one was $110
and the highest was $139. That lower one was the
big house with the columns. I think you can see it
from here, from out front."

"This house is clean," says Mom, as though
Dickey has said it was dirty.

"Yes, ma'am," says Dickey, "and people
really like that. It makes them think it's been taken
care of."

"Well, it has," says Dad, defensively.

"I can see that," says Dickey. "Did you have
an idea of what you wanted to ask?"

But they don't respond.

"Now, if we use that average for, say,
eighteen hundred square feet, that would come out
to about $230,000." I can already see Dad's eyes
going wide behind his glasses. Mom lets out an
audible "Oooh!"

"This house is bigger than that," says Dad,
harshly.

"I was just using that for an estimate," says
Dickey. "Whatever it turns out to be. Did you have
a number in mind?"

"We're not going to give it away," Mom says
in her harshest tone. You can always hear Mom
when it concerns her money; otherwise she squeaks
and grunts pitifully.

"We were thinking near three hundred," says
Dad.

Dickey pecks on his calculator. "Why don't I get my counter and I'll go outside and get us a square footage number. Is that all right?" but he's already getting up from his seat. "I'll be right back," he says.

"Do you need any help?" I ask, but he declines as he goes out. I take the papers he's left behind and look at them. "You know, Dad, even if it's two thousand that would be $150 per square foot. That's a lot more than any of these."

"This is a nice house." He turns a page upside down, tilts his head, and then turns it back. "We've really kept it up. Your mom cleans on it every day."

"Let's see." I begin to calculate. "If it's eighteen hundred square feet then that comes out to about $170 versus the highest one here which is nearly $140 so that's 30 dollars times 1800 or fifty-four thousand dollars more than the highest one here. Would you pay fifty-four thousand more just because the house was clean?"

"I would," says Mom.

"No, Mom, you wouldn't pay fifty-four cents more. Both of you better get reasonable about this or tell Dickey to go away. Do you understand me?"

"Now, hold on, Sissy," says Dad. "We just want what's fair."

"Then, there shouldn't be a problem," I say. "You don't get to say 'I want this much more for my house just because it's clean.' My goodness you could have the entire house painted and all the floors replaced for ten thousand dollars."

I stop and try to remember some exercise
from one of the books that might help me get them
thinking straight, but I can't come up with
anything. My choices right now are – Move or I
walk. That's how it has to be. Brenda can fool with
you. We'll see how you like that, depending on Ms.
No-show for your taxi service.

The good news is that Dad is looking at the
comparables. Maybe he'll come to his senses, but
even if he does, Mom rules. It's always been that
way. Well, fine. They can sit out here and die in
the house, and we can read about it in the paper. I
can imagine the headline – Old Farts Croak. And
the sub-caption – Daughter Gives Up.

Dickey has returned and he's calculating and
drawing on graph paper that magically makes the
lines straight. We're all watching him like it's the
Lotto drawing. "That bump-out on the master has
to be counted," he says, and goes back to his
calculator. "I come up with eighteen-sixty which is
what it says on your PVA report."

"Eighteen-sixty," I repeat, so there's no
mistaking what he said. Mom and Dad are quiet,
then Mom starts chirping.

"What PVA thing?" she asks.

"Oh," says Dickey, "that's the website for
county property valuations. It lists all the property
in the county and tells what the property is and how
it's valued for property tax purposes."

"What's it say?" Dad wants to know.

"I've got it here," says Dickey. He passes a
copy to each of us. I'm reading it; "Stanley R. and
Gladys E., Ray." It gives their address and a bunch

of other numbers. In the Sq. Ft. block it shows, "1860". At the bottom in bold numbers it gives the value of the property as "$188,910".

He takes them through it, finishing with, "That's the value they use for taxing your property, there at the bottom."

"How'd you get this?" Mom wants to know.

"Off the internet," says Dickey.

"They didn't ask us," says Dad.

"I'm sorry?" says Dickey as he glances at me.

"How'd you get our information?" Mom accuses.

"It's a public site," says Dickey, defensively. "Everyone's tax information is on there. Anyone can get it."

Mom lets out a forceful shuddering groan. Her mouth is wide open as though she'd been caught naked in the produce aisle.

"You mean the neighbors could get this?" asks Dad.

"Sure," says Dickey, "anyone with a computer and internet access can go to the county's PVA website and find this information. It's public information."

"How they know that number?" asks Dad, accusingly.

"Which one?" asks Dickey?

"I thought it was bigger than that. How'd you all measure that number?"

"They didn't measure it, Mr. Ray. They took it off your closing statements when they were filed back when you bought this house in, let's see, 1986. Don't worry about that valuation number;

they're always behind. It'll go up for whoever buys your house when they know the selling price.

"So let's see," he continues, "eighteen-sixty at a hundred and thirty per square would be $241,800. Just going by that, I'd say a good starting price would be two-forty-five or something like that. How's that sound?"

"That'd be good," I say. "It'd give them some room to negotiate," and I look at them. "What do you think?"

Mom's too mad to think, and Dad's too shocked, so they sit there for a few moments contemplating this avalanche of depressing information. For Dad it's probably the realistic number that bothers him – more like two-fifty instead of three hundred thousand. But I know Mom, and for her it's finding out that their personal financial information is available for anyone to see. I could have guessed her next comment.

"Can you get this information on Jim's house? Or the Walkers, beside us?"

"Yes, ma'am," says Dickey.

"Mom," I say, "I can get that information on anyone. If you want me to, I will."

"I printed out your street – Sycamore – and two others," says Dickey. "Let's see," and he flips through his papers. "Here it is. Broadleaf and Poplar. Does Jim live on any of those?"

"Poplar," says Mom excitedly. "They live on Poplar."

"Jim and Lisa Canes," says Dad. "But I don't know if it's C or K, Jim Canes," and he seems to be caught up in this too.   It's as if knowing a neighbor's tax information is only fair – a way to get back at them. I could kiss Dickey for being so thorough.

"Here it is," he says. "Jim Kaynes," and he spells it, "K-A-Y-N-E-S, Kaynes. I didn't print off the whole page so I only know the tax value from this. Two-hundred sixteen thousand nine hundred and forty," he says. "That's what they're taxing him on."

"More than ours?" says Mom loudly as though she had been unjustly and grievously insulted. "Ours is better than theirs."

"It sure is," says Dad. "His yard is terrible. He moves that boat around on it all the time. They've got that wrong. They've got everything wrong. Damn it!" I know he's really upset because that's the first curse word I've heard him utter in years.

I start to explain, but Dickey takes over. "You're probably right," he says. "These numbers have more to do with when the house was bought. I'll bet he hasn't lived there very long. Do you remember when he moved in?"

"Three years ago," Dad says. "I know it was."

"Yeah," says Dickey. "Like I said, when you sell they'll use the selling price for the new tax number. So a lot of times this tax number depends on how long ago the house was sold. They're always behind on valuations. That's why yours is so low, because you bought it twenty-something years ago."

"We're not behind," shouts Mom. "We pay our bills."

"Yes, ma'am," and Dickey's taken aback. "I'm talking about the county being behind, not you. They don't raise the value as fast as the true market value goes up. That's what I meant by behind."

Poor Dickey. He's starting to get it.

"It makes me wonder what else is wrong," says Dad. His face is all scrunched up, and he's fighting to keep his glasses in place.

"What about the Walker's" asks Mom? "I guess their house is worth more than ours too because they've only lived here for a couple of years. It ought to be the other way around," and she moves forward in her seat to make the point.

I can't help but aim a told-you-so smirk at Dickey.

"Two-twenty-one," he says.

"See," Mom says to me. "And we're lower than that."

"Mrs. Ray," says Dickey, "those numbers don't have anything to do with the value of your house. In my judgment this house should go for two-thirty-five to two-forty."

"That's not much," says Mom quickly. "Not much." Silence falls on the room.

Dickey looks up and gives me a slight nod. "You don't have to decide today," he says. "Why don't you take some time to look at all this? You can call me if you have any questions about how things would work. Commissions are three and three, that's three percent for both agents assuming two are involved. If it's just me, it's four."

"So the Walkers paid two-twenty-one?" asks Dad.

"That was probably the selling price," says Dickey, "unless they've raised their valuation since they bought it."

"Can we raise our valuation?" asks Dad.

Dickey looks at him and then laughs as if Dad has made a small joke. "Well, Mr. Ray, it would just cause you to pay more property taxes, and it wouldn't do a thing to raise the price of your house. I'm sorry, but that's just how it is."

I know that Dickey can't decide what manner of beasts he's dealing with. They're sour, greedy, impolite, nosy, and stubborn, and these are their good points. They're also befuddled, prideful, and vindictive. I should be embarrassed and I guess I am, but thankfully they're old.

I use my parking spot behind Dickey as an excuse to leave when he does. When we're out of sight, I call to apologize. He lies and pretends to deal with worse, but what bothers me is that they can – and probably will – be worse.

Chapter 3: Hives or Hemorrhoids

It's summer and Theo's schedule is more flexible since school is out. He's acting dean of the School of Physical Sciences. Acting is a euphemism for lower-paid. Still, watching him come and go as he pleases, it's a wonder they pay him at all. What a job.

We're in the middle bedroom on the second floor, our library. It doesn't look like a library in a home magazine – it looks like a working library. Books are everywhere, strewn about on the desk, horizontal on shelves in front of other books and stacked on unused chairs. He's a typical messy egghead.

He moves a few journals, sets the coffee tray on the table between us and pours me a cup.

"Thanks," I say, as he bends to give me a kiss. "Are you going in today?"

"Couple hours," he says as he settles in. He grabs the handle on the recliner and rockets the footrest out.

"Must be nice," I tell him.

"Could be you," he says, "if you'd put that chemistry degree to some use." His long arm feels around on the floor beside him and retrieves several files.

"Sure. I've forgotten the difference between an acid and a base. Still looking for a new professor?"

"Yeah, there's got to be somebody."

Brian, our youngest, is in competition for a job at CERN in Europe. Theo's convinced he's leaving.

"Are you going over there today?" he asks while pouring himself a cup. He drops in two cubes of sugar. "Shit, I forgot the spoon." He grabs a pencil and stirs with the eraser end.

"No way, the bananas should last until tomorrow."

"Hear from Dickey?"

"No. I guess I should call him. They'll never sign."

He opens a file but looks at me. "You never know. Don't give up. You're not the only one dealing with parents like yours – or even worse, I'm guessing."

"My God, I hope not. I feel sorry for them, if they are."

"Stick to your guns." He shuffles through some pages. "They'll come around."

"I'm actually praying. That's bad – praying they'll move. Think if something happened to you or one of the boys."

He laughs and drops one folder to the floor. "What do you mean?"

"I mean I've used up my requests — used them up on Mom and Dad."

"I don't think it works that way. I'll bet God can handle multiple requests."

But it's me I'm worried about, not God. I'm worried that I've used up all my sincerity. Any more worrying and I'll have to take a Xanax. Even worse, I'd be taking one on my off day.

Theo goes back to his files, and I go back to staring out the giant double windows towards the house across the street. I know I'm in trouble when relief comes from thinking about which area of our hundred year old house I should clean today. My bliss is interrupted when the phone rings.

He rolls his eyes upward and gives me his best early-morning smirk. "Oh, I wonder who that could be?

But it's not Mom or Dad, it's Brenda.

"Is she coming over?" asks Theo as I hang up.

"She wants to talk to me about something. She'll be here in an hour or so."

"This can't be good," he says. "We're her relief valve."

He's right. We've noticed that, unless she's between husbands, we never hear from her.

"It's money. She's going to hit them up for money, and she doesn't want me to interfere. That'd be my guess – car problems."

"She's got more than car problems," he says, taking on a pensive look. "How long since Chester?" he asks.

Chester was her last husband – number three – and ten or fifteen years older than her.

"A couple years — I'm not sure, really. We're not even sure they're legally divorced."

He lays the files on the floor beside him and runs his fingers through his accidental Einstein hair-do. It looks like he's calculating. "Let's see, first there was Billy. He looks pretty good, in retrospect." He chuckles. "Remember when he went to the doctor and came back and said he either had hives or hemorrhoids?"

A grin creeps across my face. "I always liked him," I say. "He was kind of, well, dumb, but nice."

"Yeah," says Theo. "How did his boss put it? They were working on that house." He twists around in his recliner and crosses his bony legs.

I start to chuckle. "He said Billy was a few shingles short of a roof."

"Right. I can't believe you remember that. It's got to be, what, twenty years ago, something like that? And then there was Tom. Hell, I can't remember why *he* left her."

"Same as Billy, just up and gone. According to her she hasn't seen Billy or the kids for a couple years, but the kids see Billy all the time. Go figure that out."

"Yeah," says Theo. "If she doesn't see them, how does she know? She's the queen of inconsistency. I can't remember Tom's last name."

"Johnson," I say to myself before turning toward Theo. "Tom's last name was Johnson. Remember, Brenda said he was the best karaoke singer at Shadowlounge Bar & Grill. That wedding cost us an entire set of bedding – including a nice comforter. I'll bet it's still in Tom's sleeper-cab."

He nods. "And then the old guy, Chester. Your sister's something." He drops the footrest with a bang. "So you think she's going to try to get some money from the otherwise brutally frugal Stan and Gladys?"

"She better not ask me for it," I say.

"You got that right. What do you think they'll do?"

"Same as always. They'll give her something. She'll feed them a line of bull, and they'll write her a check. It's always for *the rent* or *the gas bill* or *a doctor* or something. She never tells them the truth – 'I found some good pot, but the dude wants me to buy the whole bag.'"

I set my cup down as Theo stands up. "You taking off," I ask?

He smiles down at me, perfect teeth white against the craggy parenthetical lines that frame his mouth. "Do you want me here for this?" He tilts his head slightly. Gray hair is puffing out of his tee-shirt, and his boxers are twisted around as though his privates are off-center.

"Up to you — wouldn't blame you for leaving."

"Well," he says, "I need to get in there sometime today, but I'll stay if you want me to."

"No. Go on. I'll take notes and file a full report when you get back." Then I add, "Take a damn shower first."

"Right," he says. "Call Dickey if you get a chance. Or I can?"

"No. I'll call him. You better get moving; you never know about Brenda; she could be here in ten minutes or six hours."

I dress, grab the coffee tray and go downstairs. I hope she comes before it gets too hot outside. She smokes up a storm, and I'm planning on us sitting on the screened-in sun porch.

I make another pot of coffee, fill Theo's insulated go-cup and kiss him goodbye as he races out the door. Must be nice to be a man – ready for work in twenty minutes.

I straighten the porch, and then sit at the kitchen island waiting for my little sister. I'm thinking about her husbands and how strange it is that we never knew why they bolted. Billy was the one we knew best. They were married for about fifteen years. For the first ten, Mom and Dad kept their kids nearly every weekend while they did something important like go to a movie, or wash the car, or hit the country music bars. They always had time, but they never had money. In fifteen years, they traded down in houses three times. When I met Chester it occurred to me that Brenda was also trading down in husbands.

The only real constant in Brenda's life has been her job as office manager for a trucking firm. Her company has been bought, moved, changed names, gone bankrupt, re-emerged and, somehow managed to keep on trucking. And she's managed to keep her job.

I'm dreading to hear our doorbell. It's as old as the house and sounds like a terribly bad electrical short. For all I know, that's what it is. It buzzes as long as you hold your finger on the button. We run to the door to get it to stop.

Buzzz! Buz! Buz! Buzzzzzzzzz! There she is.

I can see four slivers of her face through the beveled glass windows in our front door.

"Hey, Brenda, come on in." She's smiling like she's won the lottery. Her face gets chunkier every time I see her.

"Hi, Sis," she says. "Where's Handsome?"

"He's at school. Learning something I hope. Come on," and I wave her through to the sun porch.

I grab an ashtray off the server in the hallway and follow her out. I slide it across the table.

"Thanks," she says. She shakes a cigarette from the pack. "God, it's hot." She lights up, blowing a huge plume into the air.

"We can go inside," I say half-heartedly.

"No. It feels good out here. I love that big fan." She looks at the ceiling fan that hasn't been turned off since last winter. Then it dawns on me that she should be at work.

A momentary shudder runs from my head to my toes. God, has she lost her job?

"What are you doing off today?"

"I just took a day. Cecil's in Phoenix this week and Tonya's in so I decided to take off. How you guys doing?"

It's hard to concentrate with all her cleavage staring me in the face. I'm well endowed, but nothing compared to Brenda.

"Fine. Everybody's good."

"I know Brian's back. Where's he staying?"

"He's got an apartment above Kim's café over on sixth near the statue. You know, the one with the big spike thing?

"By the entrance to school?"

"Yeah. It's nice. Great big place. He says he can't hear any noise from below, but it's busy. I think they open at like five in the morning."

She's gotten bigger over the last three months. Her shoulders slope down gently curving into her arms. Tiny beads of sweat speckle her upper lip. She grabs a napkin from the holder and blots her face.

I'm wondering if I should ask about her kids. It would embarrass me to say that I haven't talked to my children for months. I don't want to punish her, but it seems unnatural not to mention them.

"Have you talked to Bobby or David?"

"Not since the last time I was here. Bobby was working for that restaurant, and I think David was still in the jewelry store."

That's the same thing she said last time. Fine, I've done my duty.

"Sorry I couldn't take them the other day," she says. "My car's been acting up. It might be the injector things. No telling what that'll cost. But, it ran today, so that's good."

They told me she had a migraine, she says it was car problems. Who knows?

I look at my empty cup. "How about some coffee? It's fresh."

"Nah. Got any Bloody Mary mix?"

"No. Sorry."

"Grapefruit juice?"

"Yeah. I thought you weren't supposed to drink that?"

"A little won't hurt," she says, so I go in and mix her a drink.

Brenda and I are so different – as though we came from different families. She's short and heavy, and she hated school. I was a nerd – took all the science classes. I used to babysit for her occasionally, but Mom and Dad didn't go out much. I like to think that I was a good sister, but we didn't have a lot in common. I always thought she was sweet, but now I'm not so sure.

When I come back out, she's on her cell phone.

"That's good," she says. "I'll do a half. Tell him to drop it at the warehouse. It'll be a couple of days. Okay," and she flips it closed.

"Tonya," she says to me. "She's getting me some stuff. I swear I can't sleep without it. It's cheaper than sleeping pills and it's not addictive. Let me know if you want a couple."

We haven't accepted her offers for the last twenty-five years. "No thanks," but then I have a stab of humility. "I already drink too much."

She stubs her cigarette out, coaxes the last one out of the pack and wads the pack up. "Mom and Dad are real upset about moving," she says. "They called me last night. I guess that guy, Dickey something, came by with some papers. Do you know?"

"Dickey Jimenez," I say. "We knew he was going over, but I haven't talked to them today. Did they sign?"

"I think so, but Dad said Mom was fit to be tied. She's blaming it on Theo, of course." She swabs her neck with the damp napkin then dabs it under her puffy eyes. "Poor Theo, he even gets blamed for the weather. Anyway, looks like it's going to happen. Let me know if you want me to do something."

I guess I have to look at the good side; Brenda's no help, but at least she isn't fighting me on this move. I can understand her position; she dare not piss them off since she might need a monetary favor.

I stand, tip-toe, reach the short string and turn the fan on high. "If they'd hire somebody to do things they could stay there, but I'll be damned if I'm going to pay someone. They can afford it, but they won't."

"I know." Her eyes follow me as I sit. "What size are you wearing?"

"Uh, I think these are eights." I look down at my shorts and straighten my tank-top. "Why?"

"You just, you look good. I like your hair, blonder like that. I'm thinking about changing mine." She pulls her damp ponytail around and holds it up. "Course, nothing looks good in this weather." She slings it back, raises her head to catch the breeze, and lets out a sigh. "Have you talked with the Beeler's people?"

I ought to say, "No. Have you?" but I won't. She's not the one carting them around. She's not the one they call about meds, or car wrecks, or groceries, or doctors. She's the one they call to bitch about me – by way of Theo.

It's a fight to keep from telling her that some help would be appreciated. I understand that she works, but one Saturday a month is not too much to ask. Not only that, but Mom and Dad want to see her. She depends on them, and they like that. It makes them feel needed. But I've tried before, and Brenda can become unpleasant – fast.

"Sally, the woman who runs Beeler's, called a couple of weeks ago," I tell her. "They had two units open. I'm keeping my fingers crossed. It's the best place. Close, and later on they can go into assisted or even the rest home."

"That's where they ought to be now." Her short chuckle is throaty. "I told them that last night so at least they know I agree with you. I wish I could help more, but work and everything." She keeps aiming that cigarette at her mouth and then moving it away.

"The thing is," I tell her, "I've got time to help them, and I don't mind, but they're as cantankerous as anyone I've ever met. It just gets to you after a while."

"I know," she says. "That's one reason I stay away. I have to be totally blapped when I talk to them. You sure you don't want a couple of doobies?"

"No. I have Xanax," and we laugh as she finally gets the cigarette to her mouth. "Anyway, it'll be better if we can get them moved."

"Well," she says, "I wanted to let you know about something." She lights up, takes a deep drag and exhales quickly. For a moment, she looks like the north wind blowing from the corner of an old map. "I told them last night that, you know, I wanted to help out more. But my damn car only works half the time. Leon's had to pick me up a couple times already, for work. Cecil's pissed off –

I've been late. Anyway, I'm talking to them, and
Dad says I should get another car. So I say, 'Sure,
Dad, I'll just write them a check.' And he says,
'Well, your mother and I could help out,' and I'm
like, 'Great!' So I wanted to let you know that I'm
going over there today. I don't know what 'help
out' means for sure, but I've got to do something."

"Good luck," I tell her. "Let me know what
the turnips say. It'll be a miracle. I told Mom the
other day that they should get one of those small
electric shredders, but she says they're too
expensive. Did you know she cuts their name and
address off their mail before they put it in the
garbage? Then she cuts the labels into little-bitty
pieces."

"You're not serious," says Brenda.

"No. For real. Dad says her hands are so bad
that she dreads doing it. He said she cried and cried
the other day, but she wouldn't let him help."

"Why's she doing that?"

"She thinks that somebody might get into her
garbage and find their name on something."

"So what?"

"So? It could be a way to rob them. I told
her their name and address was in the phone book,
but that was different, she said. 'Everybody's in
there.'"

Brenda's laughing. Her rotund body is
shaking and she chokes on her smoke. I hand her
another napkin. She coughs into it and carefully
folds it up before turning serious. "You know. We
might have to do something. I mean, they're not

really all there. We might have to take over everything."

I'm not sure what she means by 'we', but I'm damned sure not going to share guardianship with her. That's all I'd need: "I'll have to clear this with Brenda." If I can get them moved, maybe I won't have to fight that fight.

"Anyway," she suddenly stands, "if you'll get me another for the road, I'll head over there — or try to." She puts her cigarette out.

"The Bimmer is in the garage if you want to take it. You can bring it back when you're done."

"Better not," she says. "They'll know I've been over here. Plus, Dad will want to take a look at mine. You know how he is."

"It's up to you."

"Nah, it's running now. I better get going before I run out of gas."

"You mean it's outside running right now?" I probably have a shocked look. I hope some bum hasn't relieved her of it.

"Yeah, it does better when it's hot. I'll turn it off over at their place. If it doesn't start, it'll help my – my situation."

She follows me into the kitchen and watches as I pull down a Styrofoam cup and fish out a black plastic lid.

"Have you gained a little weight? Mom said you were so thin, but I think you've gained some. Bet Theo's happy." A devious laugh escapes her pouty lips.

I think I've just been damned with faint praise. She's not going to make it in the diplomatic corps. "I'm about the same, it's just moving around." Then the part about Theo hits me. "And Theo was happy before, thank you."

Oh," she says like she's just remembered something, "have I told you about Darnell?"

"I don't think so," I say while mixing her drink.

"He's the dispatcher on afternoons. We've been seeing each other, you know, a little bit."

Where do you find men named Chester and Darnell today?

I smile. "Do I smell some romance?"

"Well," says Brenda, and she pushes out her enormous breasts, "let's just say he's into the full-figured woman." She gives me a peck on the cheek. "Maybe I'll bring him over someday. Theo will like him. He's funny as hell. He must know a thousand jokes."

"Sounds great," I lie as I follow her through the house.

"Maybe we can have some dinner?" she says.

"Sure."

Finally, she's out the front door and I can hear her car chugging and shaking.

"You do need to have that fixed or something," I call as she goes down the steps.

"I'm working on that." She gives me a wink. "I'll let you know how it goes," she says as she climbs in. It's a small car, a burnt red Subaru with gaudy chrome parts, and it scrunches down when she sinks into the seat.

Darnell for dinner. I watch as she empties a cup from the window and throws it into the backseat dump. She replaces it with the vodka and grapefruit.

She pulls off, waving. She's left a big oil spot on the road out front. I go in to get some newspaper to soak it up. Theo and I both park out there.

I have a wonderful family. Darnell sounds like an interesting addition, and I'll be so excited to meet him. I still have most of Mom's pills. Using a gun would cause a big mess.

Chapter 4: Dinner with the Sheldons

Theo and I are entertaining our best friends tonight. Deidra is an accountant, and her husband, Sheldon, teaches with Theo. They're over here a lot – once a week at least – for dinner, or we'll walk to a restaurant. They've heard all about Mom and Dad.

We're sitting at our dining room table, an old mission style oak with three leaves that take it from medium to large to huge to humongous. In humongous mode some poor schmuck is sitting in the foyer. But it's as small as it gets now, which still leaves room for booze and snacks, napkins and paper-plates, and a low table decoration of scented candles.

Eventually, Mom and Dad's name comes up and Deidra asks about them.

"And how are Stan and Gladys?" She's shaking her head in mock despair.

"Ask Theo," I tell her. "He saw them last."

We smile at Theo in anticipation.

He's changed clothes from his school uniform – khakis' and a polo shirt – to baggy shorts and a physics tee shirt with "Leptons and Bosons and Quarks – Oh My!" stenciled across the front. He's wearing new glasses, the squared-off style with hardly any rim, mounted securely on his prominent beak.

He sits up straight. "I believe I can sum them up in one word," he pronounces professorially, "curmudgeons."

"Curmudgeons," repeats Deidra with an accent on each syllable. She rattles the ice in her glass and Sheldon scoots a bottle of Glenmorangie to her. She adds a little.

"Of a pestilential variety," he adds pompously.

"So, you were over there?" says Sheldon. "I didn't think you guys were on good terms?"

Theo's buddy, Claude Maynard Sheldon, is cursed with given names he doesn't like so he's always gone by Sheldon. He's not especially fond of that one either. He's the picture of a science nerd – short-sleeved white button-up shirt with a pocket protector and a half-dozen writing instruments. He's proud of his pocket protector collection – says they're getting harder and harder to find.

"Sheldon," says Deidra, "you know they love Theo." She turns back to Theo. "Don't they, Theo?"

"They think of you like a son, don't they, honey?" I add.

Theo's nodding his head and smiling. "And they even have a nickname for me – Thief. I'm Theo the Thief. Stole their little girl and led her into this life of sin." He raises his wine glass.

"What the hell were you doing over there?" asks Sheldon.

Theo motions toward me. "Saving Sissy's sanity. Took Stan to his cardiologist. Cute little fellow named Ariswamy. Ran some tests on Stanley's ticker. Damn thing was working fine." He pulls the bottle of Shiraz from a wet terra cotta cooler, and mimics Dr. Ariswamy as he pours.

"'Eeeze okay. No blockage. Ever-ting look okay. Eeeze's good.' Just my luck. Can't catch a break."

We're all chuckling at another one of Theo's piss-poor imitations of immigrant English.

"Maybe she'll go first," says Deidra.

Theo and I are both shaking our heads. "No way," and I take the bottle from Theo and put it back in the cooler.

"She's too mean to die," says Theo.

"He gets that from his side of the family," I tell them. "His grandmother lived to be a hundred and five. Legend has it she was mean, but it was a cute mean. That's different."

"Besides," Theo continues, "where would Gladys go? Nobody wants her in heaven or hell."

Sheldon thinks that's funny. He raises his glass. "Well, she can't stay here forever, can she?"

"Did she go with you and Stan?" asks Deidra. She likes to know the particulars.

Theo feigns shock. "Are you kidding?" he says. "I asked her, but she said, 'No. I need to stay home and adjust the temperature as the sun goes up.' I said, 'Well, Gladys, that sounds like a full time job.'" He looks at me. "Place was still an oven. I don't see what keeps them from passing out."

"Well, they are drying up," I tell them.

"Have you taken him before?" asks Sheldon as he adds more scotch to his glass. He drinks a lot for a little guy. I can usually tell how much he's had by the distraught condition of his comb-over.

"I took him to his Coumadin check," says Theo looking at me for confirmation, "maybe a year ago. It scared the hell out of them when they answered the door. Sissy calls them now so they don't fear for their lives when they see me coming."

"I used to think my mom was a pain," says Deidra, "but they take the cake." She removes her glasses, and lays them on the table.

Deidra is a sweet Slav, stocky, with a broad flat face that might be considered plain, except that she has the best complexion, naturally tanned, smooth, but with Santa Claus crinkles radiating from both eyes. Her smile stretches across her entire face revealing bright-white teeth all the way back to her molars. But that smile hides a biting wit.

"I don't see how you do it," Deidra continues. "Oh, how did the trip to the attorney go? Did they make the changes to their will?"

I tell them all about the aborted trip to the lawyer's office and the real estate situation. "Our agent, Dickey, dropped some papers off the day before yesterday, but they haven't signed yet, as far as we know."

"That business with the will would bother me," she says. "I think I'd call that lawyer of theirs and see if he won't tell you what's going on. I'll bet he'll go Judas on them if you'll schedule a paid hour. Hell, for all you know, he's the beneficiary of the damn thing."

"That's crazy," says Theo. "They're leaving it all to the Society for the Preservation of Satanic Rituals."

Deidra looks at him. "I rest my case."

We talk for another hour or so, mostly about boating. They have a boat named *Aquantum Leap*, a forty-seven foot Chris Craft. According to Sheldon, she was built before the industry used sophisticated computers to pare down the amount of fiberglass needed to assure perpetual buoyancy. He says she's a dock-crusher. We've gone out with them on weekends, and sometimes we'll stay on it at the dock if they're out of town.

Sheldon stands and stretches. He grabs their glasses and heads into the kitchen for more ice. When he returns, he's holding one of my books on dealing with the elderly. "What's this you're reading?"

"How to Dope your Elderly Parents."

"How to cope?" he asks.

"No," I tell him, "this is the sequel."

"So first you cope, then you dope." He smiles as he pours scotch into their glasses. He sits, thumbs the paperback to the middle, and reads aloud: " *Information is vital. It may be helpful to have your parent or parents do some research on the Internet."*

He glances up at me, derisively. "Have you had them do some internet research?"

"Sure. Like my parents have a computer. They can't operate a garage door opener with one button."

I get up and empty the bottle of wine into our glasses, grab the chiller and head to the kitchen. I can hear Theo finishing his story about Dad's stress test when I return.

"Anyway," says Theo, "we get back to their house, and I follow Stan inside. He stops in his garage. He wants me to see if I can get his mower started. I say 'Stan! You're not going to mow. It's a hundred degrees outside. Plus, they just gave you a shot of something for that test. You need to hire somebody to mow or you're going to kill yourself.' So I follow him inside and there's Gladys."

Theo shakes his head and grimaces in a demonstration of despair before continuing. "So I'm standing there telling Gladys what the doctor said, but she doesn't care about that. She wants to know what it says on the toothbrush she's holding. I say 'What?' and she holds it out to me. 'What's it say?' she says. So I look at it, and it says Can Tops. I say 'Can Tops,' and she turns around and grabs a cup full of toothbrushes. 'Find the grout one,' she says. So I take the cup from her, and it's got five or six toothbrushes in it. There all marked. One says 'Kitchen grout.' One says 'Bathroom grout.' One says 'Window Sills.'"

"You're joking," says Deidra as she puts her glasses on.

"Oh no he's not," I interrupt.

"What the hell's 'Can Top' mean?" Sheldon slides the book away.

"It's the one she uses to clean off the tops of the cans. Like a can of corn or peas," I explain.

Sheldon's jaw drops. "That's a serious psychosis there."

"No shit," says Theo. "So I find two with 'grout' written on them. I say, 'Bathroom or kitchen?' Gladys says, 'Bathroom,' and I hold it out to her. She takes it, turns and heads down the hall. She hasn't even said one word to Stanley. She's got to get that damned bathroom grout cleaned."

"You have to wonder if she even cares about his test or anything," I say. "I just don't —"

"Oh," Theo breaks in. "Sissy, I forgot to tell you what happened next. I turn around, and there's no Stan. Then I hear something. I follow the sound out to the garage, and there he is — trying to start that friggin mower."

Deidra lets out a gasp, but it doesn't surprise me at all.

Theo continues. "I say, 'Stanley! What did I just tell you?' But he keeps pulling on that cord. So I walk over, point at the sparkplug, and say, 'Do you know what this is?' and he says 'sparkplug.' I say 'right.' And I reach around and grab a wrench off his workbench. I pull the plug wire and take out the sparkplug."

"You didn't," I say.

"Yes I did," says Theo as he stands up. He reaches into his pocket and pulls out a wad of paper. He unwraps the sparkplug, leans across and lays it on my placemat.

I cover my mouth. "I can't believe you did that. What'd he do?"

"Nothing. So I follow him back in . . ."

Theo goes on telling the tale, but I'm transfixed by the vision of that sparkplug. It hits me like a sledgehammer. I hear Theo, but I'm not listening to him. I'm concentrating on that insulated conductor. It has such a fascinating electro-mechanical shape; the white ceramic with the silver-ish top and the steel-looking bottom; that little hooked piece that makes the firing gap; the tight threads perfectly encircling the middle below the hexagonal nut.

It reminds me of watching Dad work on the mower. I thought we had a normal life. But now, when I think about my parent's paucity of friends or interests, I realize they never had either. Could that be why I want them to move to Beeler's? But maybe they don't want friends, and mid-eighties is probably not a good time to start. No, I want them there because it's close. Or maybe I want them there for both reasons, and for their own protection. I don't want them there just as a convenience to —

"Sissy." It's Theo's voice.

"Are you with me?"

"Sure, yeah."

All three of them are staring at me. "What?"

"You had a blank look there for a while," says Deidra. "You okay?"

"Yes. I'm fine." I look around at Theo. "So you were saying?"

He glances at Deidra and takes a drink of wine.

"I was telling them that your dad followed me out to the car. He says 'Sally,'" and he looks at Sheldon and Deidra, "that's the lady who runs Beeler's Trace, 'is pretty nice.' But the whole time he's whispering so Gladys can't hear him. He's terrified of her."

"That's for sure," I agree. "Hey. We better decide where we're going to eat before we can't

walk." I look across at Deidra, and then focus on
Sheldon. "And you two better stay here tonight.
Okay?"

"Whatever you say." Sheldon downs the last
of his scotch. "So they know the people at
Beeler's?"

"Yeah," I tell them. "They've been over
there a dozen times in the last ten years. They've
pestered Sally to death. I keep telling her to keep
me posted on openings – that we're trying to get
them to move. They like the place, it's just, you
know, getting them to do it."

Deidra begins to gather things up. "Well,
Theo, do you think you'll be taking Stan for his
check-ups from now on?"

Theo stands, stretches and wobbles a bit. He
walks around the table and bends down, his hands
on Deidra's shoulders. "You know what, Deidra?
I'd rather have my teeth cleaned with the business
end of a used proctologic device than have to take
him to the doctor again."

Before Theo can come up with any other
clever images, I lead our small troupe in a quick
clean-up effort, then head us towards the door. I
already know we'll be eating at La Paloma. It's the
shortest stagger from here.

Chapter 5: Psychological Victory

Dickey called right after Deidra left this morning. Wonder of wonders, they've signed a listing contract for $252,000. Dickey says he can work with that.

I'm excited until he tells me that, surprise, Mom wasn't on her best behavior.

"Your dad said something to her about his having power of attorney," he told me. "I'm not sure what that was about?"

I explained it to him. "They must have been into a fight. He's telling her he can sign for her, and he can. Their POA's are recorded in the deed office, so he can do a real estate deal. But he never would. That I can guarantee. It's an idle threat."

Dickey is going to keep me posted on showings. He asked if I could get them to leave the house "just for a walk," when it's shown. I promise to try.

Back on the porch, I'm thinking about the whole power of attorney thing. I mentioned getting power of attorney for both of them about two years ago, and they acted like I was scheming to empty their accounts. "No reason for that," said Mom. "That's our business. Not yours or Theo's."

Dad wasn't any better; "Now hold on Sissy," he'd said. "You just take us over there, and we can sign it."

It concerned another change to their will. Their lawyer's office is about a mile from our house. The first trip they found something they didn't like. So it took two trips to get the damned thing signed. That's when I said, "Wouldn't it be easier if I had your power of attorney? I could sign this stuff for you. You wouldn't have to make all these trips."

But here's what they heard: "I've got a gun. Empty your pockets. You, lady, write down all your account numbers or the old geezer gets it. Now sign these blank checks. That's right. Very good. Now you, mister, grab the duct tape. Go all the way around her head with it. Hurry!"

The sad thing is; I'm not sure that's an exaggeration.

#

A new listing gets a lot of early interest, which is exactly what my mother doesn't want. I'm over here to take them shopping because I know an agent is coming to show the house, but Mom refuses to leave.

"You go on now," she says. "Stan can pick it up. He knows what we want. Make sure you check the dates on the milk." She scrunches deeper into the worn wingback.

Dad's pacing around nervously anticipating the coming battle.

"Mom, you're going with us. That's the reason I came over, so you two would be out of the house when they get here." I'm standing in front of her chair in the hothouse. I lowered the temperature when I came in, but Dad had already dropped it to seventy-five.

But, she's not budging, and before I can get her to the car I've got to get her to dress in something other than that faded, tissue-thin housecoat.

"Now you come on, Gladys," says Dad. "They ain't going to take anything. Nothing in here they want. Come on."

She remains defiant. "There's plenty in here. Plenty good things they might want. That dresser is an antique." She nods toward a chest that would need a mule train to cart off.

"We'll know if that's missing, Mom, and we'll sue – okay?" That's not exactly how the book recommends it, but you've got to improvise in these situations.

"Lawyers would get it all," she says, smartly. She interlaces her fingers in a show of resolve, the tissue puffing up like a flower.

It's hard to tell if she's trying to sabotage a sell, or if she is genuinely concerned about having other people in her house. It's probably both. She doesn't trust people in her house while she's here, much less when she's gone, even though no one has ever stolen a thing from her.

I shouldn't be surprised—that's the definition of paranoid/schizophrenia. I know because I looked it up and her picture is right beside the definition. She's had prescriptions to help her cope, but she's too proud to admit she's got a problem.

Her mother and sister had similar issues. Mom blamed their problems on their husbands too. "Those men were both alcoholics," she told me when I was young. I've since concluded that Grandma and Aunt Emily drove their husbands to drink. Even that didn't relieve the pain of living with them, and they both left their wives early in their marriages.

I have to be careful. The way I've been acting for the last couple of years could drive a man to drink—it drove me to it.

So I'm standing here trying to think of some way to get Mom to budge. Logic is out – it's not allowed. Then it comes to me.

"Okay, Mom. You stay here while we go shopping for bananas and onions. I hope we can find the kind you like; otherwise they'll just go to waste. All that money, down the drain. And I'm not sure we'll have time to check the expiration date on every single carton of milk, but we'll try."

Dad is standing there, helpless as a lamb. "Now come on. You go with us," he begs.

I walk over to Dad and put my arm around him. "I'm sure he's just as good at picking things out as you are, so come on." I turn Dad towards the stairway and start to head us out. But I stop short, release him and turn back to her. "One thing," I tell her, "if they don't meet your high standards then it's your problem. I've got to get back to the house, and I don't have time to take them back for an exchange or a refund."

"You know what I want." She untwines her fingers and rubs her nose. She looks up at me with hazel eyes that are beady despite their sunken mounting behind her glasses.

"Bananas, green on the edges," I say, as I move towards Dad again, but stop.

"No. No!" she says. "Green at the top and bottom. You know that." She starts to move around in her chair as if she's uncomfortable. She angrily wipes her nose with that tissue.

"Whatever," I say like a fourteen year old. "Come on, Dad." He starts, and then I stop him and look back at her. "And no brown on the Vidalia."

"Not Vidalia. They're too sweet." She scoots to the edge of the chair, her hands grasping the chair arms like she's going to push herself up.

"Okay. Just an onion, but no brown on it, right?"

"Why don't you just go with us?" says Dad. He's stuck by the stairs, waiting on further directions. "You know what you want. Come on, now."

"Bermuda," she says with a force usually reserved for financial matters. "White Bermuda. Just like always, Sissy."

"I thought they were yellow?" I'm starting to get into this torturing routine. She's shaking her head and starting to push herself up. Dad shuffles over to help her. He keeps repeating, "Come on, now."

"They're not yellow. White. White!" she cries.

I'm dismissive. "Okay Mom, white. We'll get a white onion. But it can't have any brown on it. No brown at all," I say with finality.

"No Sissy. It can have some right at the top. They all have some right at the top," she pleads.

"Top of the onion," I repeat. "Brown on top. Now what about the bottom? Can there be a little brown on the bottom?"

"It's like tan," she says. "It's not brown on the bottom," and Dad is walking her to her bedroom.

"I got it," I tell her as they disappear down the hall.

I don't want to overplay my hand here. The agent is due in about ten minutes. I hope they don't get here early.

It takes her less than a minute to get on some of the ugliest cloths she owns.

"I don't understand your clothes," I tell her. "If they're stolen while we're gone, I'd at least have on some nice ones so they can't get those." She turns around and heads back into the bedroom. She reappears in no time flat wearing the pants suit I bought her. I can't change clothes that fast. It's like Superman in a phone booth.

"Good decision," I say. "Now let's go."

Dad keeps repeating his "come on, now" mantra as we head out the door, and Mom is mumbling to herself. I keep my mouth shut, open the doors and clear the way for the car entrance performance. She's babbling away as I get her belted into the backseat. She's out of here now.

"I know what you're doing," she says almost under her breath. "I know," she keeps repeating.

I know too. I'm playing obsessive / compulsive against paranoid/schizoid. I'm already thinking of ways to reverse the order to accomplish some future objective. But I'm not going to use it at the store, as much as I'd like to, if I can think of a way. I don't want to abuse my new found sense of power.

Plus, I know she realizes what's happened, and she's trying to figure a way out. My guess is that she'll decide that whatever I want will determine what she does, since she also suffers from obstinate/asshole syndrome. I'll have to take that into consideration the next time.

I know it's a small success, but I feel good. Even Alice doesn't have a pill that makes you feel like this. It's better than remembering that it was Serrano, not Mapplethorpe, who did Piss-Christ like Mr. Know-it-all Theo argued. It's better than getting Final Jeopardy right when the brainiacs all miss it.

But I'm not going to let my sense of elation cloud my judgment in the store. Mom wants to give me a tutorial on bananas and onions, but I'm having no part of it. I'm not learning a damn thing about them that can be used against me in the future. Ignorance is not bliss, it's power.

"You just go on," I tell her, "I've got my own shopping to do," and I walk away singing that song, "How does it feel?" by Dylan, I think. But I'm substituting my own words:

> How does it feel?
> To be on your own,
> Just a shopping drone,
> And you've left your home,
> And Dickey, he's going to sell it,
> And that's for reeeeeeeeeeal!
> How does it feeeeeeeel?

I'll spare you the other ten verses I come up with while I'm dancing through the wonderful superstore.

Chapter 6: Carolyn's Dinner Revelation

I'm looking through my wardrobe for something to wear to T2's for dinner. I've learned to be careful. You feel foolish in jeans when other guests arrive in yachting attire.

And Alicia always dresses fashionably. She's about the prettiest thing I've ever seen – tall and statuesque with soft features, high cheekbones, straight blond hair with a commercial sheen, and, of course, boobs. No matter what she paid, she got her money's worth.

She's also quietly sophisticated. She seems to fit in with the well-to-do even though I know she wasn't raised in riches, just like T2 wasn't. Their life appears idyllic and that's enough to scare the hell out of me. At times she seems like the grand prize that went with the house and the cars, like T2 had won a contest. I try to look at them as I imagine my parents should have looked at me and Theo, if that makes sense. A therapist will charge more for that line.

All this is going through my head while I pick something out. I've narrowed my choices down to black or black with black piping. Never let your mood dictate your outfit or you'll wear funeral threads to a wedding. So now I'm looking to find something that I might wear to, say, a late night dinner with close friends. But that requires that I pick out a restaurant, since that would determine the clothes. To heck with it – I'm just going to put on something comfortable.

"What are you wearing?" asks Theo.

Just what I wanted — added pressure. Why doesn't he go first so I can take a cue from him? Oh, that's right. Because he's an idiot, and for proof you only have to look at what he's wearing.

"Don't you have a kilt?" I say. His shorts are bright plaid, green with jolting orange lines. A kilt would be an improvement. He gets these weird clothing ideas from the university atmosphere. I wish he would take a hint from Brian who dresses modestly and looks spectacular. Why can't he dress like that?

"Take those off," I order.

"You want to have sex again?" he asks.

"Sure, honey, I've got another three minutes. Wear long pants," I tell him. "You know T2 keeps the place like an icebox when it's this hot. That's why Ali has to wear a sweater."

"I hope she doesn't wear anything under it," he snickers.

"She's your daughter-in-law, you sick-o."

"Wait a minute now," he says. "In some cultures that gives me first dibs."

"Theo, the culture expert. The one who thought Carmen was about an elephant. Put on some long pants."

He does as ordered and I'm waiting to see if his choice gives me any direction. I try to be inconspicuous.

"You're never going to let me forget that, are you?" he says. No, but even if I did there's still plenty of other examples to choose from.

"That's better," I say as he picks out a pair of cream colored dress pants with pleats.

"They match my flowers," he says pointing at the giant print of his Hawaiian shirt. It's the same shirt he intended to wear with the baggy green and orange shorts. That shirt should have sued him for slander.

He walks over to the massive wardrobe that supplements my small corner closet. "I like this," and he points to a faded denim skirt that I should have thrown away ten years ago. He's such a help. "Or this." That's a better choice, but I think the tropical print goes a little too well with all the tropical plants she's spread around the house.

"It'll look like I came in camouflage."

But it does give me an inspiration and I put on a Leopard print top with beige shorts. It's not perfect, but I've avoided another near disaster. How long can my luck hold out?

#

We're on the road in Theo's Escalade, or as I refer to it, the Chrome-mobile. He says it's more appropriate than the Honda at T2's house.

T2 and Ali live in a McMansion neighborhood. It's like a subdivision raised to the third or fourth power. It's amazing that so many people can afford these massive houses. It seems like every street has an empty guardhouse at the entrance. They must be planning ahead for an attack. All the utilities are underground and every yard is spotted with pear trees.

"Is this it?" asks Theo. I'm the navigator in our lives. Theo is the driver.

"It's left on Chartridge," I tell him.

"How in the hell am I going to find it when the signs are done up in Paleolithic Greek script mounted on the corner on the other side of this stupid median."

Theo starts bitching as soon as he gets in a car. He has zero tolerance, especially for other drivers, and I'm constantly warning him to calm down or else he's going to have a heart attack. And I don't want that while I'm riding with him. Anyway, just to give you a flavor of riding with Theo, I'll list some of his more common rants:

-- It's the pedal on the right, dumbass.
-- That stalk on the left is the turn indicator, moron.
-- signal before you brake, bonehead.
-- Cut in front of me, then turn, asshole.
-- Take your time – we don't want to make this light, jerk.
-- Q-tip alert – cottontops ahead. Prepare for slow.
-- This would be a nice place for a road.
-- It's your turn, jackass.
-- They're waiting for a written invitation, go on.

You get the picture – if he's in a car, he's in a hurry. But his best tirades are situational.

We come to a stop sign and he reads the sign below it: "'CROSS TRAFFIC DOES NOT STOP.' Why doesn't the cross traffic stop?" he says. "Can't see shit here, but the cross traffic doesn't have to stop. I guess they want T-bones at this intersection. Too many humans. Too many humans. Let's kill some off at the intersection."

He takes a deep breath when we finally turn onto Winsome Way and pass mansion after mansion.

"Look at that one," he says. "That's ten thousand square feet of ugly. What were they thinking?" He goes into his acting mode. "Oh, Catherine, I found some crappy brick and we need so much of it. Let's use it." Then, in the woman's voice, "Okay, but whatever we do, let's don't break it up with nice looking windows." He shakes his head in exasperation. "Damn windows look like portholes on a homemade houseboat. Idiots."

Compared to most, T2's house is nice looking. It's a tropical design with lots of stone and stucco. We couldn't afford his driveway. It's stamped concrete with colored pavers every ten feet or so. It's circular, passing under a portico. Theo pulls through and parks in one of the spaces marked off by brown pavers.

The front doors are decorated with cut-glass palm fronds. Sparkling beveled windows frame the doors and look into the foyer. The doorbell is on a pull cord that reminds me of something stolen from The Addams Family. Theo gives it a couple of sturdy tugs and a few seconds later Ali glides across the black and white squares of marble dressed like Marilyn Monroe, only pink instead of white.

"Whoa," says Theo just before she opens the door.

"Hi," she says and gives him a quick kiss. She gives me a hug. "Come on," she says, "T2's in the kitchen. It's so hot," and we follow her in.

"Hey, Pop," says T2. He closes the wooden refrigerator door and gives me a kiss. "Mom, you look great. Are you riding your bike again? You look like you've lost some weight." He heads over to the back counter.

"I might have," I tell him, even though I know I'm the same. "Mom and Dad can bring on a case of anorexia nervosa in Pavarotti. That must be it."

"Can I help?" Theo goes around the counter and takes a bar-tending position. He leans across to me. "Can I get you something Ma'am?"

"Yeah," says T2. "We got a new cork puller. See if you can figure out how that thing works," and he points to a wine bottle opener that's mounted on the back counter.

"Theo will figure that out," I announce while maneuvering into a seat at the multi-level granite counter stretching halfway across a kitchen the size of Montana.

"Brian called," says Ali. "He can't make it tonight. He's going out with Dominique something. I told him she was welcomed, but I think they had other plans." She gives me a sly look.

"Other plans," I repeat, looking at Theo. "That's two weekends in a row."

"Thank God," says Theo. He glances at T2. "I was beginning to wonder about your brother."

"He's been busy," says T2. "Livermore, then back here. Now he's talking about CERN. Do you know her?"

Theo nods. "Dominique Sanders. She's Assistant Dean for Student Affairs. Been here for three or four years. Gorgeous woman. She's African-American. Has a doctorate in…"

"Finance," I finish. "International Finance. That might come in handy if she were to end up in, say, Europe."

"Oh sure." Theo gives me his patented sneer. "Like she's going to chase Brian to CERN and give up her job. Wardrow," and he looks at T2 and Ali, "that's Dominique's boss, is as old as dirt. He's going any day, and she's next in line. She's already doing his job. That's how Brian met her."

"But you never know." I say teasingly. "Never know about these things."

"I'd hate for Brian to leave again," says T2, "but if he does, we're going over to see him. I can't wait to see the collider. He could get us in."

"It's something to see—incredible really." Theo picks up a bottle of red and shows it to Ali. She nods, and Theo pops the cork out like a pro.

"We have another guest tonight," says Ali.

"Carolyn Mullins," T2 tells us. "She's with Credit First. She's head of Tech, or will be soon. But that's not why I invited her. At lunch the other day we were talking, and she was saying that her mom was really giving her a hard time." He looks at me. "I told her about you and Grandma, and I thought you guys had something in common. I hope that was okay," he says.

"Any help's appreciated," I say in Mom's moaning voice.

"I'll say," says Theo. "At least misery loves company. That's why your mom and I are so much in love."

"He's so funny," says Ali as she moves about the kitchen. "We're having prosciutto with melon, followed by . . ." and she details the entire menu. It sounds fairly ambitious for a young woman who's burnt nearly everything we've eaten here. "It was prepared at Brend-Lees," she says. "All I have to do is heat it up."

That's where she's had problems in the past, the heat-it-up part. "Oh that sounds good," I say.

I remember when I was her age, maybe a little younger, and I couldn't boil water. I once dropped a half-dozen pieces of battered chicken into Crisco that was so hot that Theo pronounced it done as soon as he rescued it from the bubbling froth of splashing oil. It was pretty as a picture and cooked about a quarter-inch deep.

When Carolyn arrives, Ali introduces her, gets her a glass of wine, and takes her on the standard house tour. I follow along, but try to stay out of the way.

Carolyn is about my age, medium height, curvy, and a bit plump. Her hair is coarse, nearly gray and I wonder why she doesn't color it since her face is full and wrinkle free. I would call her cute. She is very complimentary about the house as we progress from room to room.

When we return to the kitchen Carolyn and I sit on the same side of the giant counter and watch as Theo finishes a tutorial on the pneumatic cork remover.

"You can't really experiment with this thing unless you're planning to drink a whole lot of wine," he tells the group. "We should get one, Sissy."

"Oh, you mean it works on screw-tops too?"

"Sure," says Theo. "And on box wines," he adds.

We spend the next twenty or thirty minutes talking about Carolyn's bank and some of the people who work there, and then about the university, but mostly about T2 and Ali's house. Finally, Ali, T2 and Theo start doing some serious food preparation, and I turn to Carolyn.

"I'm sorry to hear you've had some difficulty with your mom," I say. "Mine's about to drive me crazy."

"Yeah," she says, "she's kind of demented, if you know what I mean. Not Alzheimer's, I don't think. And stubborn. Oh!"

"Same with my parents," I say. "And mean. They can be mean. It's something."

"And my brother," says Carolyn. "He's absolutely no help. He gets upset over the least little thing, then disappears. Leaves me to take care of her all by myself until he decides to show up again."

"I've got a sister. She's pretty bad, but" and I lower my voice "she's not beyond 'borrowing' some of Mom's pain pills."

Carolyn nods. "Tell me about it. That's the only time Darnell shows up, to 'borrow' some money." She laughs and takes a drink of her wine.

Oh my God—it can't be! Two Darnells! I'm sitting here thinking about what to do. Should I ask or should I keep my mouth shut?

"This house is really something," Carolyn says looking around.

"Yeah, they're doing pretty well." But I'm not involved in our conversation now, I'm just thinking *Darnell*. Theo, T2 and Ali are oblivious. They're fooling with the food and joking around, and Theo's telling them a story about T2 and Brian when they were kids.

I'm wondering what to do. Do I even want her to know if it's the same Darnell?

I'm going to ask. I guess I have to. What do they say, honesty is the best policy? And I have to think about Carolyn? It's not fair to her, really. I've got to find out.

"Your brother's name is Darnell?"

"Yeah," says Carolyn. "You don't hear that one much. I hate to say it but he's pretty much a low-life, even if he is my brother."

I've got to do this now before she says something else she'll regret.

"Is there any." I stop. She's looking at me. I'm not sure this is how I want to ask. "Any chance Darnell works for a trucking company?"

Carolyn's head pops up, and then her whole body tenses. "You know Darnell?" she says with enough surprise that the other conversations stop.

"Is he a dispatcher?"

"Yes." Her dark brown eyes are wide open and her mouth forms a perfect O. "I can't believe that you know Darnell."

"I don't know him," I add quickly. "I've just heard his name. I think he's dating my sister, maybe."

She shakes her head. "No. He's dating some big fat girl where he works." She looks relieved.

"Brenda," I say and everyone is looking at Carolyn.

"Oh" and she covers her mouth with both hands. "Oh, I'm sorry, I shouldn't have said that."

"Is it Brenda?"

Carolyn nods from behind her hands.

"My God, they're dating," I announce to her and the rest of our small party.

"Brenda's dating her brother?" Theo is looking at me.

I nod.

"That's so sweet," says Ali. "What a coincidence. Major. Very major coincidence. It's serendipitous."

Well, this falls into unplanned discoveries, but fortunate is debatable.

"Oh please don't tell her I said that," begs Carolyn.

"Don't worry. She'll never hear it from me. You know what she told me?" I'm looking at her to see if she really wants to hear this, or if she really wants to leave.

She nods, cautiously. Theo, T2, and Ali are all leaning across the counter.

"Ali!" I point to the cooktop. "That's starting to smoke." She turns, sets the skillet off the burner and goes back to looking at us.

"Brenda said." I try to stifle a laugh. "She said that he was into the full figured woman." We start to snicker, but we're watching Carolyn to see how she's taking it. At first she looks shocked. But slowly her smile widens and she starts to let it go. Soon we're all laughing.

Ali mimics Brenda by shoving out her breasts, puffing her cheeks and swaying side to side.

Carolyn is still trying to cover her mouth while laughing harder and harder. "You know," she says, catching her breath, "his first wife was bigger than Brenda," and we all start laughing again.

"He's downsizing," says Theo and, well, it was one of those nights that can never be duplicated. We laughed, talked and tried to figure out what we were going to tell them. Finally, we decided that it was probably best to mention our dinner to Brenda and Darnell like it was just a happy little coincidence quickly forgotten.

But Carolyn and I promised to stay in touch and keep each other posted.

Chapter 7: Surreptitious Banditos

I'm sitting on the sun porch which is not a porch and gets no sun. Maybe it was a sunny porch a hundred years ago, before it was incorporated into the house, and before those huge trees in the backyard grew to be a hundred feet tall, and before those houses behind us were built. But it's not sunny now, which is good, because it's been so hot. But this morning it's comfortable, and I'm drinking coffee.

I love living in town. Theo and I both grew up in outer suburbia right next to Outer Mongolia. I can't imagine that we'd ever go back out there even if we could afford T2's house.

Everything here is close. If it weren't for Mom and Dad, I could almost operate on a bicycle with a big basket. We can walk to at least twenty different restaurants, and we're starting to show the results of their proximity. Theo keeps talking about joining the Downtown Athletic Club to get some exercise, but talk is cheap and the club isn't.

It is still early when Brian shows up. We sit at the dining room table and I catch him up on our dinner at T2's. Wow, is he a hunk. There was nothing like him when I was in school. Well, Theo maybe, but Brian's better looking and better built. And smarter, says Theo. He doesn't even act like it bothers him to admit it.

Brian is picking up some papers for a "surreptitious markup" according to Theo. They're playing a trick on Sheldon. Theo returns from our library and hands over a block of paper like you'd buy for a printer. It looks like a lot of work for a joke, but Brian doesn't seem to mind. Physicists. Go figure.

I'm half-listening to them talk about Brian's posting to CERN in Europe. They're not sure when it will happen, but Theo still hasn't found a replacement to teach Brian's QCD class.

"What does QCD stand for again," I ask as Brian stands up to leave.

"Quantum Chromodynamics," says Theo.

"Now does that have anything to do with the Escalade?" I deliver one of my most mischievous smiles.

"Ha, ha, ha," says Theo derisively. "Very funny." He turns to Brian. "Your mom's a regular comedienne."

Theo puts his arm around my shoulder as we follow Brian to the door. He gives me a squeeze. "Imagine, Sissy," Theo enthuses, "twenty-five hundred physicists in one place."

"Sounds like the most boring spot on the planet," I concede.

"Asshole." He pushes me away, kiddingly, before looking back to Brian, who's laughing.

"She's mean," says Brian.

"It's from dealing with the gruesome twosome," says Theo.

As we're standing at the door saying goodbye, the phone rings. I give Brian a quick hug, and dart for the phone. It's Dickey. Theo comes back out on the porch and listens as I talk. When

I'm through, he says, "That sounded promising from your end."

"Yeah, can you believe the house showed three times yesterday? And there's two scheduled for today. Dickey says Mom and Dad sat in lawn chairs in the garage. He thought that was okay, but the couple who looked at it first, when I took them to the store, are coming back tomorrow. He says they'd like some time so they can take measurements."

Theo's brows are arched. "Oh, that's good. They must be serious."

"The guy's parents live on Holly, so a block over. His mom baby-sits for them." I'm so excited that I have to consciously relax my fists.

Theo's really smiling now. "Good. Good," he says. "Damn, that'd be nice – sell that baby before your mom even knows what hit her. Did he say anything else? I thought you said something about an offer?"

"I think he's saying that they might offer low, just so we won't be surprised." I grab the carafe and pour us some coffee. I'm shaking, and the coffee seems to quiver into the cups.

Theo stretches his arms wide, leaning back in his chair. "I'm warning you, if they get anywhere close to reasonable, that place is gone. I don't care if I have to make up the difference myself – it's gone."

That sounds crazy, I think to myself. They'd find out. But why didn't I think of that?

"You're not serious, are you?"

"Damn straight I'm serious," says Theo. "Think about it. You go over there an average of, say, two-and-a-half times a week. So that's twenty miles each way, plus wherever you take them. So fifty miles per trip, right? There's all that gas, plus your time. Plus, maybe we can get rid of a potential visit to a shrink." He jabs me playfully in the arm.

"But how much would we go?"

"I don't know, whatever it takes; we'd have to decide."

It's so bad we are apparently willing to buy them out of their house. Theo's a pretty good mathematician, and he's thought about this.

"Does Dickey know about this?"

"No, but he'll have to find out. Maybe it won't come to that. Maybe your parents will come to their senses and realize they don't have another choice."

Sure, Theo. You know how I know they won't do that? It's simple; that's what they SHOULD do.

#

I've hatched a devious plot to get them out of the house. It involves installing irrational fear into Mom about murderous thugs lose in a nearby (eight miles away) neighborhood. It'll take some time to germinate. I justify it by pointing out that it was on the front page of the second section.

She's in a foul mood. I put my purse down on the kitchen counter and look at my watch. We've got plenty of time before the couple and their agent are due here. I try to dampen the opposition with a compliment.

"The house looks nice."

"Same as ever," she shoots back, quick as a gunslinger, "except your dad cleaned up in his room." She mutters something bad about "Stanley" just below the comprehension threshold.

I know I need to deflate the animosity before I move further into my cruel plan, but something happens when I follow Mom down the short stairs into the hothouse room. It's like a blast furnace that smacks you in the face, and it makes me mad as hell that they won't turn the air down, and then they force me to sit in here, and I've just had it.

Dad is following, when I stop and turn. "I can't handle the heat in here. I'm going back to the kitchen." It's tiny, but since they've shrunken to Thumbelina size I estimate that three of us can get around the small table permanently pushed up against the wall.

I feel bad immediately. Dad doesn't know which way to go, but I guess his sense of politeness causes him to follow me. The square table has three chairs, and I take the furthest. Dad stands against the counter, undecided. I get up and start opening cabinets searching for a glass. Of course, I know where they are, but the sound of someone looking through her cabinets is enough to move her crooked butt.

"What are you doing?" she calls loudly. I can hear her moving our way. "I'll get it. I'll get it," she shouts, but she's too late. I grab a precious plastic cup, throw in a few cubes and a splash of water and reach my seat before she can intercept me.

"I got it," I call out. Dad takes shelter in the corner as she hurries round the doorway.

"Oh, Sissy," she says sharply, "I could have done that. You let me do that."

What she means is, "You touch another one of my glasses and I'll slit your throat!"

"Mom, it's just a glass of water."

She's in a bad spot now. She wants to be stubborn and go back, but she can't leave me in here where I might touch something else. My foray has scared the hell out of her.

"Oh," she moans. Then she turns on Dad. "Well, sit down, Stanley. We'll just sit in here until they come."

Dad squints and moves into the chair to my right.

Mom sits across from me. "You didn't need to come over today. We don't need anything from the store. My goodness, we were just there." Then, under her breath; "I don't know how often you go. I guess when *he* needs something."

Apparently, I only go to the store for Theo. I am able to exist without any store-bought goods. But I keep telling myself I'm not here to challenge her. I need to keep my eyes on the prize.

I try to be optimistic. "Sounds like you've been busy – five showings in two days."

"Uh, we stayed in the garage with the doors open." Dad says this while looking at Mom to see if it's okay to pass along this vital information.

"You mean the big door?" I ask.

Mom's twisting her tissue into a knot, still furious we're in the kitchen.

"Uh, well…maybe both. Both doors."

"Isn't it hot in there?" I look at Mom, forcing her to respond.

"Not if you open it up," she says defensively.

"It's pretty hot," says Dad as he stands. "I better open it so it'll cool down some."

"Yeah," I say. "The clients might want to measure in there." I've got plenty of time to work on them so I'm trying to be patient.

"Why?" asks Mom.

"Well, maybe they want to see if their car will fit."

"It's a garage, Sissy. It's made for cars."

I can see that she intends to take an obstinate position on everything. It's her way to prepare for the upcoming fight, like an athlete doing stretching exercises.

"A lot of people drive trucks today. They're longer than cars and wider too."

I can hear the garage door going up. When Dad comes back into the kitchen it's as if he brought the Mojave with him.

"I'd hate to have to pay your cooling bill." I'm going to let that percolate in her scheming little brain. "Did you talk with any of the lookers?"

"Yeah," says Dad, "some nice people — young people. Last couple had some kids."

"They can't afford this house," says Mom. "None of them could, that I saw."

"Well, come on now. You don't know," says Dad. "You can't tell just by looking these days, you know that don'tcha?"

"I can tell," says the soothsayer. "Not one of them."

Dad holds his ground, since I'm here to protect him. "The one feller worked for the airport. That's probably a good job. Why else would they come?"

"That's what I want to know. Why'd they come? Can't look really, with kids. I never," she finishes.

I knew that was coming. It must have been torture for her to sit out there while kids roamed around her house.

"How long did people look around?"

"Not very long," says Dad.

"Stanley! Why, they were here for a long time." She goes into her mumble routine. "Probably went through everything we own." Then she sits up straighter. "They could be seeing what we have. Come back to get it." She wipes her nose, satisfied with her conclusion.

Everything's quiet while Mom makes nervous clicking sounds with her mouth. "Stan," she orders, "go close that door to the garage. Our air conditioner will be running at midnight."

One seed has matured.

I try to change the subject. "Brian may be moving to Europe for a while."

"Brian," says Mom. "Where is he?"

"Mom," I say with full exasperation, "he's been here since last December. He was over here a month ago. He offered to mow, remember?"

Dad returns from the Mojave shut-down assignment. "Yeah," he says. "I remember. How's he doing?"

"Good. Like I said, he might be moving to Europe. Sounds like a pretty big job."

"Brian," says Mom, very low and she's looking at the table.

She's probably trying to remember him. Brian looks too much like Theo. She may recall that they're in the same line of work, but whatever it is, she's cast him from her mind like a bad dream.

I remember, years ago, when he was in high school. Mom and Dad were at our house for some reason, (it couldn't have been to eat because we're not clean enough) and Mom discovered that he had to wear dress clothes to school.

She went into a real fit. "I don't understand it, making them wear a tie to school. It's just silly. How's that help learning? They can't be comfortable dressed like adults. Probably won't learn anything. I never."

Brian defended the dress code. "I think, Grandma, that they want us to be serious about it. It's not that big a deal, really."

"Well other kids don't have to and they get an education too. It's just for show, that's all."

Brian was familiar with her uncharitable attitude so he just said he had some homework, and took off.

But I knew what it was all about.

My Mom, and by force of habit if not conviction, my Dad, resented almost everything about our lives. She resented our independence

both financially and socially. She resented our kids
and their success in sports and school. She resented
our house, which was way too big, and who'd want
to live in something that old anyway? She resented
Theo and his job at the university and his trips
abroad to conferences and collaborations. She
resented our vacations and Theo's sabbaticals,
which were always more work than his job. She
resented everything, but especially me.

I've tried to figure out what happened to
cause her to be like this. I know it had to do with
control. When I married Theo, she lost control over
me. That, really, was my big sin. She took her
anger out on all of us, but especially Theo.

"What time is it?" she asks, as though the
thirty-year-old wall clock isn't working.

I look up. "They'll be here in a half-hour."
I'm tempted to issue a "should" statement about the
air conditioning, but I resist. "Anything else going
on?"

"Brenda was here," says Dad.

"Oh!" screeches Mom. It's her way of saying
that it's none of my business – it's private. She's
admonishing Dad to mind his mouth.

That simple "Oh!" says a lot about my
family. Normally, I'd say, "Yeah, she stopped by
my house too," but not today. For some reason
we've devolved to the point where a sibling's visit
is a family secret.

"How's she doing?" I ask.

Silence. Mom's not talking and Dad's afraid
too.

"Well?" I ask. I take a sip of my water. I look from her to him.

He pushes his glasses up, takes a deep breath and says, "Her car's not working right. I looked at it. She needs something newer."

Mom brightens, changing the subject. "She said Bobby was still in the jewelry business, and David is running some kind of a phone company. They're doing fine."

I'm not going to tell her that even Brenda doesn't know how they're doing.

"That's good to hear," I say, and I plug for Brenda. "I knew she had some car problems. You're right, Dad, she needs something newer, or needs to get hers working."

"She weighs too much," says Mom as though Brenda's weight somehow has a bearing on the car situation. But since she's knocked on Brenda, she needs to mitigate her comments by saying, "She's not naturally tall and skinny like you."

"I'm not skinny, Mom. I weigh 150." I want to add 'naturally', but I don't. "She say anything else?"

"She's worried about work. I don't think that guy likes her," says Dad.

"What guy?" I ask, but I know it's Cecil. I caught that when Brenda was over.

"Her boss," says Mom. "He's some kind of a nut."

Well, at least I'm hearing it from an expert.

"We might have to help her out some," says Dad.

"Some," she mumbles.

"That'd be nice of you," I say, but I immediately regret it. In my ears, it has the ring of "unusual, but nice."

"But," says Dad, and he looks at her, "whatever we do for Brenda, I think we should do for you. Else it's not fair."

My God, do I detect a hint of decency? That remark tells me a lot: first, they've actually talked about something other than the faults of humanity. Second, I'm not sure what "help" means, just like Brenda wasn't, but it sounds like more than a tune-up. And third, they've actually taken me into consideration. I'm starting to feel guilty about mentioning the criminal duo.

"How far is it?" she asks.

"What?" I ask.

"Newland Heights."

That's where the big murders took place. Now I do feel bad. I've got to come up with a better plan than trying to incite irrational fear – in my parents, for God's sake! The Big Guy won't like this. I've decided to play it down. If they won't leave the house, then that's the way it is.

"Eight or ten miles. Why?"

"They could be over this way." Her sunken eyes seem to light up.

"Oh, Gladys," says Dad.

"Mom, there's fifty or sixty thousand houses between them and you. I doubt if they're going to show up here."

"We don't know who these people coming over are," she says.

I'm so stupid that I continue to be rational. "Well, a man and a woman with a real estate agent don't fit the bill of particulars."

She stands up abruptly. "Just two men," she says.

"What?"

"Just two men are coming. The woman is at work, so it's just two men. We don't know them. It could be anybody." She points a boney finger at me.

I do believe that one more rational argument from me, and they'll be racing out of here. So I'm caught betwixt and between. But, since I continue to be optimistic in the face of all contrary evidence, I decide to try to help her realize that she's acting crazy.

"Come on. You should hear yourself. Those bandits are not coming to this house. You're being irrational now."

"No I'm not," she says, pacing in a circle. "Happens all the time. You see it on the news." She's wringing her hands.

Meanwhile, I'm thinking biblical, as in, "See what thou hast wrought?" I decide on a new tactic, one I should have come up with before.

"Well, I just thought that we could get out of here while they measure. You said you needed a new prescription for your glasses. I thought we'd get that done. They might be able to do it in an hour. That's what they advertise anyway."

"I need some too," says Dad, and I can see the hope in his face. I also know his glasses are only two months old. She was supposed to go with

us then, but her migraine kept her here. I don't
know whether he's crazy, or if he's trying to help.

"You're crazy," says Mom, and I guess that
answers my question. "I need some though. We
could probably get them now, if Sissy doesn't mind
taking me."

"No. That'd be great. It's a good time to do
it." I push away from the table a little bit. I don't
want to act too anxious to get them out of here. If
she remembers, she'll buck me in a second.

"I need my purse," she says.

"I'll get it," and Dad practically bursts from
the table. He better settle down or he's going to
blow it. He disappears down the hallway toward
the garage.

"Where's he going?" I ask her.

"It's in the garage. We hide it in there. I tell
you, his memory has gotten so bad that I know he
won't be able to find it. And we just put it in there,
right before you came."

But she's wrong, and he returns with the
purse. She doesn't say anything as I help her get
her housecoat off. She's wearing one of those
pants-suits I bought her. Dad's attired in his bum
outfit. I guess you can get by with it if you're his
age.

We were gone about two hours. A note on
the counter from the real estate guy said, "Thanks.
We'll get back to Mr. Jimenez. Have a nice day."

That's a pretty nice note for a couple of
banditos.

Chapter 8: A Bawling Oasis

I'm pulling a Mom-and-Dad—sitting in our dining room at the big table watching for Brenda's arrival. It's been nearly a week since that first couple took the measurements. Yesterday, after looking at "every house in the plan," according to Dickey, they made an offer. Two-forty — twelve grand less than the asking price.

I phoned Mom and Dad, and you'd have thought that this couple had called them a string of foul and contemptible names. I tried to reason with them.

"I'm not giving it away." said Mom.

"It's worth more than that," said Dad. "Way more. We told that Mexican guy no. We're not taking that, you know that don'tcha?"

"It's ridiculous," said Mom. "I never."

Dickey would be surprised to learn that he's Mexican since his grandparents hail from Chicago. He practically begged Mom and Dad to make a counter-offer, but they're insulted, he said. He thought it had to do with the reality of possibly, actually, selling the house. "Trouble is," he told me, "they've got to respond in twenty-four hours, or the offer expires."

I think Dickey was embarrassed to call me. Maybe he felt he should have been able to make them understand that this is the way the process works—offer, counter-offer. But he's worried. "There are three other houses in the subdivision. These people have some choices. I think they like your parents' place because they can cut through the yards and get to Grandma's. But I don't know if that's enough. It's not a bad offer. They've sold their house. They're ready. It'd be a shame to let it go without at least a counter."

Theo was dancing around the bedroom last night. As far as he's concerned, the house is sold. "Twelve grand," he said. "That's do-able. They'll come up some. That's their first offer. You need to get your parents to come down, counter. If we can get them three or four thousand apart, then we'll just slide in there and write a check. Yippee."

I've never seen someone so happy to give away several thousand dollars. I feel bad about that. As far as Theo's concerned, if it helps me, it's worth it. I worry that they'll find out. But also I'm mad because they have the money to take this offer and move on. If Dad has his numbers right, they actually make more money than they spend. And I'm supposed to chip in several thousand?

I called Brenda last night and told her what was going on. She's supposed to "take a day," to help salvage the deal. They'll be more likely to see the light if she's with me.

It's debatable whether or not she'll show up. It was like talking to Giggles, the Laughing Doll last night. She was as bubbly as champagne. I don't know if she was on something, or what.

The phone is sitting right beside me when it rings. I look at the number. It's Bubbles, so I know she isn't going.

"Hello, Brenda."

"Oh, hi Sissy." She sounds like she's talking from the bottom of a well. "I tell you. I just can't make it today. My head is hurting so bad. I threw up this morning. Sorry."

"Migraine?"

"Yeah, they come and go. I never know what triggers them."

I want to say that she should suspect whatever it was she was on last night, but I don't want to rock the boat. Still, it's damned irritating. I took half a Xanax early, and I already know I'm going to take another half before I leave – and a go-cup full of white.

"That's okay," I tell her. "I understand. But it's a great offer. These people have already sold their house, so it's not contingent on that. I've got to make them see."

She goes into to her apology routine, again. Then she says, "Darnell may have to take me to the doctor. We'll see when he gets up."

So that tells me that Darnell is living there, or staying there, or whatever. I haven't told her about the Carolyn connection. I've decided that if she says something, I'll say "Oh yeah, I forgot. We met…" and let it go. Maybe I'll call Carolyn tonight and file a report.

Meanwhile, I leave to save the deal. It's still early and the traffic is murderous. I can't believe that my parents moved way out here. Somehow, my mom had it in her mind that this neighborhood had a better class of people. It's as close as you can get to her hometown of Harmon and still be in the county, and obviously, the very best people are from there. That's where Grandma lived and died.

Ditto Aunt Emily. Mom and Dad have burial sites there, next to Grandma.

I'm thinking about how sad it will be at their funerals. Theo's family will attend, and that's it. Stan and Gladys don't have a single friend here – or there. Brenda will bring her friend named Darnell, if he's still around. As little as we've seen of her kids, Bobby and David, I don't even know if *they* would come. It's a crying shame, and if I'm not careful, I'm going to start crying.

I'm on that stretch of Sixty-eight that has a rise crowned by the ubiquitous traffic signal. From here, I can see at least two miles down the road. What a horrid mess. I've counted before and there are about twenty traffic lights in front of me, a gauntlet if you will. Sixty-eight's a five lane here and both sides are cluttered with every business known to mankind.

Theo jokes that the best-looking buildings along here are the strip clubs. There's a dozen spaced over several miles. One of them, Oasis, has palm trees decorated during Christmas. It's the prettiest display.

There are no interstates within fifteen miles of this place except the one about four or five miles past Mom and Dad's, but I'd drive fifty miles to connect with it from where we live. It's tempting from the top of this hill.

And it's tempting to turn around. My sense of dread is palpable. I guess it's God's way of reminding me that everything in the world isn't perfect, like my life was going to be. Theo and I were planning to travel in the next year or so. We were really going to see the planet, but we're no closer to that than I am to an interstate.

We've reached the point where we don't even talk about travel like we used to. I'm not worried that Theo's going to leave me for some traveling trophy wife, but at the same time, it punishes him. My parents are punishing Theo, through me. Punishment in absentia. I'll bet there's a Latin legal term for that – torturo absentio, or something.

Speaking of torture, I'm within thirty lights of the split-level elders.

#

The door swings open as I reach the stoop.

"You're early," says Dad.

"Must be something," Mom mutters from her position behind him.

"Yeah," I say, "but traffic was terrible." I decide to try a play on her pity. "I'll be so glad to get you guys' closer. I don't think I can handle another day on that road."

"Come so early," moans Mom. "Could have waited…not going to give this away." She groans into the kitchen.

"I've got some errands to run later," I say. "I have a house to take care of too, you know." So this has started out great.

"Guess Theo can't help," she says as she hunches even more than usual. It's like she's expecting an incoming barrage, and she's taking cover. She's standing in the corner of the kitchen protecting her plastic glasses.

I want to blast her mean old ass, but I take a few deep breaths, just like the books say. "Calm down," I tell myself. As soon as I get them moved, I'm going to start shilling for the drug company that makes Xanax or a wine company that produces a cheap white.

"Well," I say in as perky a voice as I can muster, "you've got an offer. It sounds pretty good."

"Now you just wait on that, Sissy," says Dad. "It's no good. We talked about it last night, you know that don'tcha? It's too low."

He's been cowed into submission by the Wicked Witch of the West, but he better not mess with me. I benched a hundred pounds ten years ago which means I can easily kick his scrawny butt all over this house. And after all that traffic, I'm in a good mood to do it.

"They'll come up. That's how it works. They know how to play the game." I put on my best happy-face like things are just wonderful.

"Two-forty," mumbles Mom. "Just want to steal it is all."

"Okay, Mom. I get your position. Now let's talk about a counter offer. Dickey says it's a clean deal – no contingencies. They've sold their house. They need somewhere to live."

"You tell her." She turns toward the sink, but glances over her shoulder at Dad.

Even I can feel the intimidation. "See here, Sissy," he says. "Asking price was too low. Now they want us to go there. That ain't fair. It's two-fifty-two. That's the price. You know that don'tcha?"

What I know is that both of them understand what's going on. I can't do much more than state the obvious. "So you listed at two-fifty-two, and you don't plan to consider anything below that? You should have listed higher if that was your bottom number, but, of course, nobody would have made an offer at a hundred-forty a square foot."

I exploit a short silence. "Mom, can I have a glass of water?" I hope this concession will distract her.

"Oh yes. I'll get it," and she fetches a scratched-up plastic glass, fights with the ice cubes, fills the glass and sets it down in front of me. She moves back to her corner.

I take a drink. "Thanks. You know, even at two-forty you're doing better than the average per square foot, probably because the place is so clean and well maintained."

"A hundred-twenty-nine," she croaks.

She's not only rational, but precise, when it suits her.

"Why don't we counter at two-forty-eight," I suggest.

"Now, there's no need to counter," says Dad. "Wait for another offer. No hurry. We're not in a hurry, you know that don'tcha?"

No shit, Sherlock, as Theo would say. I'm the one that's in a hurry. They're not in a hurry to do anything. As far as they're concerned, I can grow old on Sixty-eight and die at a friggin traffic light and right now I'm wishing I would.
There's not a jury in the world that would convict me if I strangled both of them right now! They'd

probably give me a medal. "Service To Mankind Award goes to – Sissy!" "Now, Bill, she deserves this medal. She killed both her parents who were occupying valuable space on the planet as well as some shitty real estate. Plus, they were using air. She really didn't have any close competition, Bill."

Perhaps I should re-think that promo for Xanax?

I decide to go for broke. "Look. If you counter at two-forty-eight they'll probably come back at two-forty-four. Then you can settle the deal at two-forty-six. Two-forty-six is a little more than one-thirty-two a square foot. That's a good price for this place."

"Good for them," she crows. "That's who it's good for."

"I can't believe you two," I tell them in a voice that's so calm that it surprises me. "Six thousand less than your asking price. That's ninety-seven percent of what you asked. That's pretty close. When you're within five percent, that's pretty good. Now let's counter."

But they wouldn't do it. It took me two more hours to finally get them to agree to counter at two-fifty. I called Dickey and he said he'd be over later to have them sign. I've done all I can.

The drive home is a kind of therapy. Thinking about them, I conclude something that is worse than terrible; I don't love them, I don't dislike them, I actually hate them. There, I said it. I've pushed that thought out of my mind for nearly three years, but I've got to face up to it. I hate my parents. You expect that out of the mouth of a fourteen-year-old who's been grounded, but not from a grounded fifty-eight-year old. But it's the truth. I simply hate them.

Then I have to wonder, what type of guilt would lead me to torture myself like this? What incredible perversion exists within me? Make no mistake about it, I tell myself; you are the problem in this relationship. Even Brenda can handle them better than this.

Now I'm starting to cry. No, the truth is, I'm bawling. I can't even see the road, and I've got a hundred traffic lights to go. I pull over. When I look up, I'm in the empty parking lot of Oasis, under a plastic palm tree. I suppose the girls don't start dancing this early, but then I see some guy going in. He looks just like I expect Darnell to look –thin, old, gray and scuzzy. Through teary eyes I watch him open the door and disappear inside. Does he work here? I wonder. Or maybe he's a customer? I'd have to go inside to find out. I bet they serve wine. I'm tempted.

Chapter 9: Early Mourning

Our house is warm and inviting. I'm sure others feel that way about their homes, but there's something special about old houses like this one. The millwork is intricate and painted glossy white with a grayish sheen. The wooden floors have inlaid patterns in each corner, and the built-ins have beveled glass doors. Our ceilings are tall, even in the closets, which have a tendency to collect junk.

I'm standing in the hall. My eyes are still red and swollen from my crying fit, but I've got to be strong and get through this minor catastrophe. I've been planning to reorganize our closets for years. Maybe this is the right time.

But when I open the first door, the immensity of the task overwhelms me. A survey of the contents reveals basketballs, baseball caps, gloves, coats, old dresses, light bulbs, vacuum cleaners, shoes, enough neckties to construct an escape ladder from the top of the Empire State Building, bowling balls, tennis rackets, giant plastic storage bins full of who-knows-what, table pads, lava lamps, shoeshine kits, lint rollers, fifty pair of I'll-get-back-into-these-some-day" jeans, enough towels to supply the army, eight giant boxes full of premium stereo equipment, dozens of old rugs of every conceivable size, pattern, and material, two never used ironing boards, enough chargers to make a significant dent in the power grid—and that's just the hall closet.

I release a shuddering sob as I back away. I sink down onto the hall bench, eyes fixed firmly on the task in front of me. For a moment I imagine that the contents of this closet are the big problem in my life. Wouldn't that be nice? I can do anything I want here without a single argument. Okay, basketballs, I've decided to move you to the basement. And I don't want to hear any crap. Got it?

After a few minutes, I move to the living room and fall asleep on the couch.

I'm still there when Theo gets home an hour later. I made myself a promise – tell Theo everything, no matter what happens, or how I feel about it, or whether or not it's embarrassing or painful or disgusting or infuriating. Not because he needs to know every little thing, but because it's healthy. I figure, if I get to the point where I won't tell Theo, then I'm in really bad shape.

So no sooner does he sit down than I'm into today's story about the two-fifty counter-offer, but more importantly, my bawling fit at the Oasis Strip Club.

He moves over to sit beside me. As soon as he puts his arm around me, I start crying again. He keeps saying, "It's all right. It's all right. Two-fifty's good. It's all right."

But the whole time he doesn't know why I'm crying. I'm going to tell him how I feel about them as soon as I can pull myself together. I already know what he's going to say: "You don't hate them. It only feels like it today because of what you just went through." And maybe that's what I want to hear.

He hands me his handkerchief, I dry my eyes and try to settle down. "I want to tell you something."

"You mean there's more?" He chuckles carefully. If you ever want to get Theo in a gentle mood, just have a nervous breakdown.

"I'm afraid so. I came to a conclusion on the way home. That's why I was crying at the Oasis."

His brows rise wrinkling his forehead. "I'm intrigued."

I hesitate for a few moments, staring ahead, contemplating my confession. I can feel Theo bending over to look at me. "I've decided that I actually hate my parents. I mean it, I hate them."

"Who the hell doesn't?" he asks. "I don't blame you. They're about the most despicable people I've ever met. I'm sorry to have to say that, but it's the truth. If they'd lost their marbles or suffered from some kind of disease you could understand, but that's not the case. I think you've been a real saint, dealing with them. I couldn't do it."

That's not the response I expected, and I'm not sure it's the response I want, but he's validated my feelings. He told me the truth. It's an ugly truth, but it's the truth. Theo doesn't bad-mouth Mom and Dad very often. He gets mad when they upset me, but he usually doesn't say much, just makes jokes.

"You've heard me say that I don't care if they blame me for everything," he goes on. "That's the truth. If I loved them, I would care. But I don't love them. I don't think they want to be loved.

They don't show any signs of it. I don't like to get on them because they're your parents. But honey, they're driving you crazy."

He pauses and it looks like he's trying to decide if he should go on.

"I know. I know you're right." I give him a weak smile.

"You've got to forget about the ideal loving parents. You didn't get that. But, come on, you got our family. We're not perfect either, or at least the rest of you aren't, but it's not a bad trade."

That's his idea of a joke. I let out a pitiful laugh, his signal to continue.

"Hate's bad for your health. You're going to have to move beyond it. The question is, how? How can we get to some point where you accept them for how they are, do what's reasonably best for them, and also keep your sanity? Maybe you should see somebody. It might help. For me, it's like they died years ago."

"That's amazing," I say looking up at him. "What you just said about them dying years ago. In one of my books it says almost exactly that, that people with parents like mine should start the mourning process just as though their parents died years ago. For me, it's like they started dying when we married, but it's a hard thing to grasp."

"Look," says Theo, "it'll be more convenient once they're moved, but it won't solve the real problem. I think you should tell them, 'Hey, I'm available once a week for grocery shopping or whatever. But once a week — that's all. You know how to get a cab and the Home Assist people cost

forty-eight dollars for three hours. They'll take you
anywhere and if there's an hour left, they'll come in
and clean the house. But you've got to mean it.
You can't let your mom lay some big guilt trip on
you. Together, you and I are going to move beyond
this. Okay? Together."

Boy, I needed that. And he's cheap.

He always says "together." That's so
important to me, so I don't feel like I'm facing this
alone. I wonder about Carolyn. How does she
manage? I gather she's been divorced for years.

He keeps his arm around me as we walk to
the kitchen. I pour us some wine, the good stuff,
and we talk about their house. Now Theo's up to
the twelve thousand dollars difference. "It's a done
deal," he says. "That place is out of here. Gone.
Sold to the first bidder. Terminated."

He calls Dickey. Thank God they signed the
counter. Now we've got to wait another twenty-
four excruciating hours. But it's okay; we'll wait
together.

Chapter 10: Brenda's Check

I'm in the kitchen with chimney-woman who's smoking up a storm. Clouds of billowing grayish haze circle her head like a transcendental halo from an old sci-fi movie. Brenda's hair is a bee-hive on top before turning into a modified mullet. It's so unnaturally black that I suspect it was done professionally.

She's just returned from Mom and Dad's in Darnell's "pick-em-up truck," as she calls it. It's the nicest looking vehicle I've seen her drive in fifteen years. "Candy Apple Red," she tells me. "He's so anal about that truck. Wash and wax, once a week."

If he's so anal about that truck, why's he letting her drive it? She's had it a couple hours so it's probably got a wadded up fast food bag and a paper cup lying on the floorboard in a puddle of melted ice.

It's six hours past the deadline, and we haven't heard a thing from the buyers. Dickey called earlier and said they needed more time. I busted my butt to meet the deadline, but apparently their deadline is more flexible.

Brenda's visit is unannounced. I'm pissed because she went over there and didn't do a thing except sit around and talk—no Kroger or Walgreen for Brenda. Now she drops in on us, smokes a few cigarettes, and then asks if she can go out on the porch to make a "private call."

She's still there when our phone rings.

It's Dad. He wants to discuss the milk-banana-onion delivery schedule. He doesn't know it, but my next visit will coincide with their next selling decision.

As I'm talking to him, I can see Brenda standing on the sun porch. She's got her cell phone to her ear as she takes a toke a joint. She's smoking a doobie on the porch! I'm thinking; don't worry about that marijuana plume, just stand there at the big screened windows so everybody can see. Damn!"

I try to remember that I'm talking to my father who died years ago. "Look, I'm busy now. We'll talk tomorrow," and I get off the phone. I can't mention that Brenda is here because it's a family secret. We can't let my deceased parents know that we're secretly seeing each other, plotting their demise.

Brenda was in a good mood when she got here – laughing and coughing and puffing away. She should really be a blast if she ever comes off that porch. I want to scream at her – "borrowed vehicles and borrowed time – what are you thinking? Think!" It sounds like a country music hit.

But I don't. I'm going to be polite and hope this is just a bad dream. At least I know I'm half right — it's bad.

Theo will be here soon so I move two drinks, one ashtray and a partial pack of GT One's to the dining room. He won't recognize that truck parked out front, but he'll smell her as soon as he walks in.

I hear him open the front door just as Brenda comes in the back. There's going to be a collision in the dining room. I should take cover.

"Hi honey," I say as he rounds the door. "Brenda's here," I add quickly so he won't say something stupid. "And here she is now!" I exclaim like a game show host.

"Brenda!" he says. "How are you doing? I didn't see your car."

"Hi, Handsome — come here and give me a hug."

Theo piles his briefcase and a bunch of files on the table, and they hug.

"Did you see my new sled? Come on," and she grabs his elbow, leading him. "I'll show you."

They're both gone and I'm relieved, even if it's just for a minute. I can hear them talking about Anal's truck. Theo's offering all kinds of superlatives as I hear the door. Silence. They've gone outside to look at it—another respite. The only thing better is if they decide to take it for a test drive.

But no such luck—they're back. Theo moves his junk off the table and Brenda takes his chair. It's a big wooden chair with square slats on the back and giant arms. It's the one I want her in because she's too big for the side chairs.

We have the usual family banter and Theo asks about her kids again, but gets the same broken-record answer.

I get me and Theo some wine and make Brenda another drink. Finally she says, "I've got some news." She's smiling and jiggling like Santa.

She reaches into her purse and pulls out a check. "Look at this." She seems excited as she passes it to me.

It's a check from Mom and Dad for — and I read it two or three times to make sure — twenty-thousand dollars!

"My God! They gave you this?"

"Sure did," she says, "and it gets better. Dad says that when the house sells he's going to give you exactly the same amount. Said it wasn't fair to give this much to me without also giving it to you. So, you owe me big sister. You owe me big time. Twenty grand! Not a bad haul for a couple visits."

I'm sitting here, astounded, as Theo looks at the check.

It keeps happening that I don't know how to feel, exactly. It doesn't seem that complicated. I ought to be happy that Mr. and Mrs. Scrooge have decided to part with some mullah, and who couldn't use twenty grand?

"I think they're right," says Theo. He hands the check back to Brenda. "It's only fair." He looks at me. "Let's see, Sissy, that gets your per trip cost down to nearly a breakeven. At twenty grand a year you're getting just below minimum wage." He looks back at Brenda. "I wish they'd given you her check. So ours is waiting on a sold sign?"

"Hey, it's the best I could do." Her shoulders rise and her neck disappears as she smiles.

"Are you really going to get a car?" I ask. Ooh – that didn't sound right. Why didn't I ask her if she was going to buy an old junker and blow the rest on a once-in-a-lifetime trip to the Okefenokee Swamp?

"Sure. 'Course, it might not take all of it." She winks at us and chuckles.   So, I've got the first part right. Now it's just a matter of where they're going for the trip.

"Darnell says I can get a new Kia for this. God, I can't wait to spend it. I'll show you what I buy."

"So I get paid when the house sells, is that right?"

"That's what he said."

"What did Mom say?"

"She was just bitching about the yard. She thinks it needs mowing. I told her it's going to be nothing but dust, and he better wait. Then I told her to hire somebody and guess what she says? 'Can't afford that now — not after we pay him.'" She grins at Theo. "I think she meant you."

"I ought to go over there and mow it just to show her," says Theo. Then he cackles devilishly. "Nah," he says.

We spend the next hour talking, but we can't get anything out of Brenda except that Darnell's funny, work's a bitch and Cecil's an asshole.

And then I remember Carolyn. I'd forgotten about her. I use that as justification for deciding not to mention her. If she's as unimportant as we want Brenda and Darnell to think she is, then it's easy to forget to mention her.

And I really don't want to get into that. Who knows if there'll be a Darnell in the picture a month from now? I'm just going to forget about them in all this excitement about the money.

Finally, I walk her out to the truck, and she shows me all the "after-market add-ons," that Darnell has festooned it with. She's particularly proud of the little guy on the back window who's peeing on the word "Chevy." Wow – what pride of ownership. My truck's better than your truck, my truck's better than . . .

She uses the giant chrome stepladder to leverage herself up to the handhold to pull herself in. The door's still open as she starts the engine and rolls down her window. "Hear that?" she asks. "Ain't that a sweet sound?" Damned if old Darnell hasn't turned her into a friggin' Ford feminist.

Then it hits me like a ton of bricks and I blurt it out: "Hey, you make damn sure, whatever you buy, that it has four doors. You understand me?"

"Ahhh," she says like she wishes I hadn't thought of that. "You figured it out. There goes the turbo rocket I was going to get."

Now I feel bad about being so forceful, so I cover it up. "Oh. I forgot to tell you. We went to T2's house for dinner the other day. There were some other people there—clients or customers— bank types. We met a woman named Carolyn something. Said she was Darnell's sister. We didn't talk much, but she seemed real nice. I forget where she works."

"Carolyn Mullins," she says, looking down at me from the cab. Suddenly her bubbly self has disappeared. She's got a big frown on her face. "She's a bitch. A real bitch. I've met her. First

Union, I think. She's run off three or four
husbands—wants Darnell to do everything for their
mom. Which he does, of course, 'because she's
never around. She's always going to a conference
or something, husband shopping. You tell T2 to
stay away from her. Tell Alicia to watch out, she's
on the hunt. Darnell says she screwed her way up
the ladder. I got to go," she says, and I can tell
she's mad. She pulls away without looking to see if
anyone's coming down the road. I'm left standing
here wondering what the hell that was all about.

Back in the house I'm telling Theo about it.
"Doesn't sound like we'll be having Thanksgiving
dinner together," he says. "So Brenda's telling you
Carolyn has run off three or four husbands? What a
hoot. Maybe she's jealous because Carolyn's one
up on her. She's daffy. I think she's on some kind
of drugs."

Then I tell him about the porch joint. I'm
surprised when he laughs. "She'll never grow up.
It's just the way she is. So you think they'll ever
mention the money?"

"They better – twenty thousand dollars."

"Now, here's a situation that doesn't happen
every day. We're sitting around talking about
kicking in a bunch of money to make this sale go
through, and they're going to reimburse us, plus.
What a deal. I believe this is a first. Now we've
got a monetary incentive to make this work. Your
mom was right. I feel like I'm robbing them, and it
feels goooooooood."

Well, at least one of us is in a goooooooood
mood.

Chapter 11: That Mexican Guy

The buyers finally countered yesterday, fourteen hours late. But it's worked out perfectly; their offer will expire at the same time as the milk and bananas.

I'm on my horse named Honda riding out to Fort Ray, a split-level outpost on the edge of suburbia occupied by the fearsome duo of Stan and Gladys. It's never been sacked, but it's never met a foe as determined as this barbarian and her horde.

The horde includes one Mexican and one Professor. But I'm the warrior in this battle. The Mexican's just an outrider, and the Professor guards the homeland, sharpens the warrior's sword, and polishes the warrior's shield.

I guide my stately steed down the freeway of exit strategies. I'm calm and cool as I attempt an end-around to attack Fort Ray from behind.

It's funny what your mind can conjure up while traveling down an interstate.

To avoid another close encounter with a palm tree, I've chosen to go the long way around to Mom and Dad's. This interstate route almost begs you to daydream differently than you would on Sixty-eight. Traffic is more serious, the rigs are bigger and they run faster. There are plenty of vehicles, all screaming along at seventy-four miles per hour, the feel bad speed. All of us hope that we won't get a ticket because the cop would feel bad writing one for nine miles over the limit.

The placidness of the passing countryside frees the mind to think serious thoughts. I'm thinking about victory. Wagner's 'Ride of the Valkyeries' comes to mind. Victory in this battle means getting Stan and Gladys relocated to Fort Oldies, aka, Beeler's Trace. And I can taste victory, smell it, see it just on the horizon, right up there in front of me. It looks like a million small setting suns flickering into existence. And the suns are getting closer and closer and now they're staying on and forming into lines of reddish streaks that disappear over the horizon. They're – no, wait. They're friggin' brake lights. Not suns. Brake lights!

One of the stately steeds must have mounted another one in an attempt to produce scrap metal. And all the other horses have stopped to graze and gaze upon the carnage. But not me. I deftly dodge death and dive for Exit 41.

Wow! What was in that Xanax?

Now I'm on Highway Eighty, Parkerstown Road. If memory serves, it runs over to Sixty-eight and connects at the light across the street from the Oasis Erection Club.

This will set me back another thirty minutes, but almost anything's better than being stuck on an interstate waiting for the crash-site dummies to show up and measure everything so the insurance companies know whom to screw.

Almost exactly thirty minutes later I'm sitting in the right turn lane looking directly across the street to my palm tree. I'm slightly upset because somebody has parked a clunker in my spot. It ruins the whole effect. Well, at least I know this much – it's not Darnell. I take some solace from the fact that, from here, it's only sixty-three lights to the split-level outpost.

I make the turn and head on at light speed. When I reach the outpost, I dismount and tie off Honda. I place my hand securely on my trusty sword and glide through the magic gate.

Gladys, the woman who died thirty years ago, is standing in the kitchen guarding her priceless collection of Melmac plates. Her dead partner, Stan, is shuffling around nervously anticipating the battle to come. I take a seat at the table occupying most of the kitchen.

"You're later than I thought," moans Mom as she rubs her hands and drops her tissue. It looks like it's going to be a big production for either one of them to pick it up, so I lean over, grab the tissue and hand it to her. But she won't take it. Instead she whines even more pitifully, and scoots the metal flip-lid garbage can over with her foot. Dad does the honors, steps on the footpad, and the top springs up. I drop the tissue in. "Now come here," says Mom.

"Where?" I ask.

"Sissy! Here. Here." and she points at the sink. "Wash your hands, my goodness. Wash your hands!"

She's exasperated with my lack of hygiene, as though she failed as a mother, which, from her perspective, she probably has. But, in a rare choose-your-battle-wisely moment, I go to the sink and wash my hands while wondering what the hell was on that tissue? As I get back to my seat, I steal a look at the floor to see if I can find the dreaded contaminant there, but it's clean, blue-speckled linoleum right up to the cabinets.

"I think they really want this house." I try to be enthusiastic like a preacher in a brothel.

"Well, not much," says Mom. "Who wouldn't, for nothing? If they can get it for that."

"Come on now, Gladys," says Dad as he pulls out her chair. She lowers herself with help from the table top and magically produces another tissue. She must have a box of them discreetly residing up her sleeve. Once she's in, Dad pulls his chair out and sits down beside me.

"Now, we've talked about it," he says to me.

"Told you they couldn't afford it." Mom sniffles into her tissue and wipes her sagging nose.

"Now, Gladys," he says, and I can tell that she's broken some promise about how this negotiation with their devilish daughter is supposed to go. He looks back at me. "Now they didn't want our offer," he says calmly. "So it's okay. If they don't want it. That Mexican guy is going to show it again, he says. So there's no hurry. So you see?"

I take a deep breath and come to a conclusion; I'm going to tell Dickey that they call him "that Mexican guy." I know I can't change them, so I'm going to do the next best thing and rat them out. Then I remember Mom talking about the first showings. She whispered to me, "and some coloreds came," like they were some form of exotic deep sea fish that wandered up to a beautiful coral reef by accident.

Mexicans and coloreds—it pisses me off, and for a moment I wish Theo were as black as black gets! If he croaks tomorrow, my next husband will be a black saxophone player from a New Orleans jazz band. He'll wear a lavender three-piece suit with giant gold medallions and diamonds imbedded in his teeth. He won't get out of bed until four in the afternoon and his first drink will be Old Granddad, neat. He'll have fourteen kids and fifty grandkids and a bunch of great grandkids. And they'll all live with us. And Mom and Dad will lose their court battle with me, and as guardian over their whole lives, I'll make them live with us too! So take that!

They're both looking at me. They have no clue how upset I am. Every single experience with them is worse than the one before. I'm not sure if I'm mad at them, or me. Why didn't I see this? Why do I tolerate it? Why can't I answer these questions?

I don't even care if they notice my efforts to get myself under control. I ask Mom for a glass of water, and I take a deep draw.

"Look," I say, "this is called a negotiation. This is how houses are sold. This couple has kids. They want to be near Grandma and Granddad. Let's counter again at, say, two-forty seven five hundred. That's meeting them half way. They've gone to two-forty-five, so you're not that far apart."

There's a chorus of negatives from both of them. You'd think that dropping their price by twenty-five hundred dollars will mean the difference between retirement in Buckingham Palace and sleeping under a bridge.

And all the while I'm fighting off the temptation to say; "Hey – you wrote a check to Bubbles for twenty grand – what's the big deal?" But I know what the big deal is. For Mom, it's not about the money. I'm not even sure it's about the house. It's about control. And who doesn't want to have control over their own lives? I know I do. But when you're dependent on others, you give up some control. Some people are wise enough to recognize that. Some even go so far as to be appreciative when helped. But Mom's on a different track.

It takes two hours. I almost tell them that Theo and I will make up the difference, but better sense prevails. The thought of Theo and me chucking out a couple thousand dollars to make this deal happen is so foreign to this miserly duo that there's no chance they'll ever think of it on their own, and I don't want to put them on that track.

All the while I'm waiting to hear about my check. I haven't let them know what Brenda told me. It's their money, and I wouldn't take a million dollars from them if it came with any sense of obligation.

Mom's throwing a fit, but she's trapped by my proximity to the Melmac. She can't leave the kitchen. Dad's glasses are steamed up and I'm worrying about his heart. But eventually they agree to counter at two-forty-nine. It's not much, but it keeps the deal alive.

This war has tired me out. I stand up and stretch. Mom's watching me warily, ready to spring into action at the first suggestion that I might attack the cupboards. I feint left and give her a start before leaning against the counter.

"Uh, how's Theo?" asks Dad.

"Fine," I say. Bless his heart. He's trying to be nice, but too many years with the beast has roughened him up to the point where a simple inquiry into the love of his daughter's life is an act of heroic dimensions. "He's busy at school. I think he spends most of his day politicking for Brian. He's trying to find someone to take over Brian's classes next semester. The real problem is that there's not a lot of money in it." Then I think of something. "Maybe twenty thousand a semester. Twenty thousand's not much for a guy with a doctorate, but that's what Brian was making, I think, twenty thousand. Plus his tutoring money and some outside work for some of the grant people. But he's fine," I conclude.

"Too much, if you ask me," says the sourpuss. She stands and heads to her corner.

"What's that?"

"Nothing. Are you going to call that guy?" She means the Mexican.

"Yeah, I'll give Dickey a call. He'll probably have to come by to get you to sign off on it. I'll let you know what he says."

It doesn't look like the references to twenty grand have had any affect. I grab my purse.

"Well," I say. "I better get going. Oh. I forgot," and I reach into my purse and search around until I find the pill bottle. "Here you go." I count out seven pills on the counter. "Feeling any better?"

"Not really," says the queen of moan. "Maybe a little," she adds reluctantly.   I pour the rest of the Vicodins out on the counter. "Looks like eight more. You said Brenda was coming over to take you to the drug store. Have you talked to her?" I busy myself putting the pills back into the bottle. I cap it and drop it into my purse, waiting.

"She says so," says Mom. "I guess so," and she's looking anywhere but at me. Dad's scuffing around in his chair.

"Uh, we talked to her, you know that don'tcha?"

"Okay. So she's planning on coming by, right?"

"Yes." Mom finally commits. Then she follows with, "I'll let you know." She's covering her bets. They know, just like I do, that Bubbles isn't all that dependable, even with a new car.

I busy myself gathering my purse, and setting the empty plastic glass in the sink. "Make sure she takes you to the store too, okay?"

Their response is a muffled composite of old-people sounds—some clicks and grunts punctuated by throat clearing. Brenda is an uncomfortable subject for them, and for me.

I decide to let it go. I just want to get back home.

Or, at least to the Oasis.

Chapter 12: Parable of the Mongrel

Theo's as happy as can be. He called Dickey and informed him that the house deal is going through even if we have to make up the difference. He sits across from me at the small island in our kitchen.

"Did he act surprised?" I ask.

"A little. I guess he can't understand why your mom and dad aren't tickled with two-forty-five, since it's a clean offer. But he knows how your mom is, so he's like, okay, I understand." He frowns and shakes his head. "So your parents never brought up your money?"

"No, and I gave them plenty of opportunities. I even mentioned twenty-thousand several times."

"I can't believe they didn't say anything," says Theo. "It doesn't look good for your, what should I call it, fair share or whatever."

Theo doesn't know it, but this has become another issue. I'm caught feeling two different ways. Brenda needs help through every fault of her own, and they're in a position to help. Why should I begrudge them that? It's their money. So why do I feel like it's somehow cheating me to give it to her and not to me? And yet, that's exactly how I feel. The fact that Dad has apparently come to the same conclusion legitimizes my position.

I'm not particularly religious, but I'm guessing that the Christian thing to do would be to pray for all three of them, then pray that I can forgive them for treating me shabbily, and then pray that I forget about it.

I don't know. That's a lot of praying.

It never bothered me when Mom and Dad gave her a couple hundred dollars every now and then, but twenty grand starts to sound like real money. So I guess I have to admit that it's not the act, it's the amount. So, where is the cut-off? How much can they give her before it starts to bother me? It would be different if she was dumped by her husband after their child was diagnosed with cancer. But twenty grand to a pothead who hasn't made a correct choice in thirty years?

It seems dirty even thinking about it, but I can't help it. On the other hand, it's not like they gave her enough to retire on. So . . .

Then I have to consider that we don't really need the money, but how would I feel if it were two-hundred thousand dollars? Or two-million? I mean, come on, how damn Christian am I expected to be?

Finally, there's the work/reward part of this deal. I do all the work, and Brenda gets rewarded for being a leach, ignoring them for years at a time, and being totally unconcerned about their well-being. What's right about that?

"What are you thinking about?" asks Theo.

"What?"

"You look lost in thought."

I explain my mixed emotions.

"Like that parable about the Prodigal Son," he says, or maybe the servants in the vineyard."

"The ones that worked different amounts but got the same pay?" I ask.

"Yeah." He stares at the ceiling for a second. "I see the owner's position on the one hand, but I see the workers position too. It's human nature to feel like you've been mistreated."

"The whole idea is to overcome that nature," I tell him. "But I see what you mean. I think the parable of the Prodigal Son is maybe a better approximation of my situation."

While I'm talking, Theo has pulled a bottle of wine out of the cooler and opens it as quickly as the best sommelier on the planet, owing to his constant practice. Theo was raised a Catholic. They must have been the vineyard workers and winemakers back then.

"Except," I continue, "in the Prodigal Son — as I recall — the father gives each son part of the estate and the younger one takes his and goes on a shopping spree. He ends up losing it all, comes home, is welcomed by the father and they give him a big party. When the older son sees this, he's pissed off. But, and this is the important difference, the father tells him that he should celebrate because the wayward son has returned, repented, AND that everything the father has will belong to him, the older son."

Theo, recognizing my relative expertise in this matter, is nodding his head in understanding while pouring wine.

"So," I finish, "the younger son who blew everything got a welcome home party, but that was all. The good son inherited the estate. But in our case, Brenda hasn't returned to the fold. She's still on the shopping spree. But she's still getting a chunk of the estate." I start to laugh. "I don't think either one of these damn parables fit the circumstances. Just my luck."

Another bottle of wine and we're both philosophical geniuses. We could talk all night and occasionally we do. It always makes me feel better, and sometimes Theo says something that actually makes sense. But not tonight.

#

I called T2 last night. I had picked up the phone to call Carolyn, but I thought I better clear it with him first. I didn't want to mess anything up. But he thought it was great, so I called her and we're meeting for lunch today at Ben's Overlook Café, just a couple blocks from our house. As I walk over, Carolyn calls my cell and she's running late.

So I've got nearly twenty minutes to kill. But my early arrival has allowed me to pick what I know to be the best outside table in the place. It's permanently shaded and has the best view of the street scene below.

And what a scene it is. This is what the city calls the Bohemian section. If you are looking for diversity, this is it. Within easy walking distance of this place there are homes worth millions of dollars and apartments that rent for three-hundred dollars a month.

I watch a woman park a Mercedes convertible while a long-haired mongrel looking guy with a backpack and a sleeping bag nearly steps into her path. I can tell he's a street bum. She gets out and they have words and she reaches in her purse and gives him some money.

I want to yell down to her that that's why they hang out here, preying on the guilt that accompanies the wealth. They just buy drugs or booze. Give it to an organization that actually helps these people.

Inside, the place is already half-full. Eventually a few people venture out into the oven that this part of the country has become. I consider going inside, but it's still comfortable at this table.

I'm thinking about Brenda's abrupt mood change when we talked about Carolyn. They must have had some kind of altercation to generate that response, but Carolyn didn't mention it. I can understand that.

And, of course, I have to consider the source. Brenda is warning me to tell T2 that Carolyn's after a new husband. Then she wants me to warn Alicia that Carolyn's on the hunt as if Carolyn presents a threat to the marriage. Brenda saw Alicia at our place three or four times. She must have forgotten. Either that or she thinks T2 has gone blind and lost his memory for God's sake.

Nevertheless, I've learned enough about quantum physics from Theo to know that improbable things happen in our world. My antennae are set on full alert.

I'm surprised when Carolyn shows up nearly on time.

"Hi, Sissy," she says. "I got out of my meeting earlier than I thought." She sits down. "It's lovely here. I haven't sat outside for a month."

She looks very professional in her banking attire. Her blue suit matches her heals. She sets her purse down beside her. I feel under-dressed with shorts and a shell, but Ben's is a casual place.

"You look so nice," I tell her. "If it's too hot, we can move inside."

"This is fine with me. Feels good here."

"It's nice as long as you can stay in the shade, and this table is always in the shade."

"Thank God," she says, laughing. "I saw Theo the other day."

"Theo?"

"Oh – I forgot. You all call him T2, but we call him Theo at the bank. I can't get over their house. I told Darnell that it was the nicest house I've ever been in, without a doubt."

"And how's Darnell?"

"Darnell is Darnell. Lazy. He's been taking Mom on a walk every day around lunch, but he gets her so upset. I don't know what I'm going to do with him. How are things with your parents?"

We order wine as I give her an update on the house deal. We talk about our parent's medical issues and their peculiarities.

Carolyn's friendly enough, even if a bit guarded. She speaks in generalities. For example, I ask where her mom lives and she says, "In town. Not too far. Not like your parents."

She has a slight accent that's hard to place, like maybe she's a second, or even third, generation immigrant. She looks a bit Mediterranean in the daylight, and she'd be much younger looking if not for the white hair. Though she's pleasant, I still haven't found out about her run-in with Brenda, if there was one. When she mentions Brenda's name, I ask her, "Now when did you meet Brenda?"

She looks up into the air like she's trying to recall. "At Mom's. I'm afraid it wasn't a very nice first meeting."

"Really. What happened?"

"I think she and Darnell had some weekend plans, like go to some cabin on the lake or something. But I had to go to Atlanta, so they had to cancel. She was a little put-off, but hey, everybody's got to do their part."

"That's right," I say. "And Brenda's not the best at pulling her share of the load. I don't blame her much though. Mom and Dad are a pain to fool with."

She takes on a serious look. "Well, Darnell's going to do his share or he ain't going to get a share if you know what I mean?"

Is she talking about his share of their mother's estate? That's all I can come up with and it seems, somehow, inappropriate to ask her what she means. If it's the estate, then she must have some control over it. Or maybe she can direct her mom to cut him out. But I'll give her credit for this, it sounds like she plays hardball with Darnell, at least when it comes to dealing with their mother.

That alone would be enough to piss Brenda off. Brenda's unconsciously selfish. It's her nature. She goes her own way and everybody else can be damned. That's how she treats Mom and Dad and it works better than my way. She got twenty-thousand dollars.

In order to prove that we aren't totally preoccupied with our elders, we talk about some other things.

She tells me how much the President of the bank likes T2. "He's got a great tracking system. It works for us, and if he plays his cards right, I think they'll buy it in Charlotte. He'll probably be able to buy ten houses like that one. I'd stay tight with him if I were you." She laughs.

When we're through, I try to pay since I invited her, but she picks up the check. "As far as the bank's concerned, I'm having lunch with Theo. You call him and tell him that he was here today." We part at the cross street.

The mongrel guy is working another woman, but I mind my own business as I cut past them. He follows me about thirty feet. "Excuse me lady," he says, but I turn on him immediately.

"No. I'm sorry. No," I say very forcefully. He turns away and heads back toward another mark.

If I were only as strong with Mom and Dad, maybe my life would be easier.

Chapter 13: Packing the Melmac

We're having a late dinner courtesy of Theo the cook. I'm sitting at the kitchen island watching him inspect the rack of cookware. He grabs a skillet and sets it on an un-lit burner.

"So, how was lunch with Carolyn?"

"Fine," I tell him. "Do you think she's attractive?"

"What?" He looks confused.

"Carolyn. Do you think she's attractive?"

He moves across from me, leans in, hands on the butcher block and gives me a quizzical look. "She's okay. Why?"

"What's *okay* mean?"

"Don't tell me you're worried about what Brenda said about T2 and Alicia." He straightens and looks at me mockingly.

"Of course not. That's ridiculous." But I can't think of why I asked the question in the first place. It just popped out. "There doesn't have to be a *why*. I was wondering, that's all."

"All right, since you're wondering." He walks around behind me, bends down with his face at my shoulder and puts his hands on my waist. He whispers into my ear, "I like a tall thin woman with a healthy rack." He moves his hands up and cups my breasts. "I'm not a fan of white hair." He kisses my neck. "I like sparkling blue eyes on a dishwater-blond."

I tilt my head back and give him a tender kiss on the cheek. "And I like a man who's full of shit.

A man who's willing to give up dinner for sex. Know a guy like that?"

He releases my breasts quickly and straightens up. "Let's talk about it after we've eaten." We laugh as he walks to the front of the island. "She's okay means that she's a seven-point-five out of a possible ten. How's that? You're a nine-point-nine."

"Aren't you sweet?" I bat my eyes.

He turns back to his work. "Did you find out what happened between her and Brenda?"

"I think so," I answer. "She says Brenda and Darnell had plans to go to a cabin for the weekend, but she made them cancel because she had to go to Atlanta."

"For business?" His brows rise.

"Could be," I say, "but how many times do you have to go somewhere on banking business for the weekend? Maybe she had a date, or she was in Atlanta prowling around for a husband, if you believe Brenda. Anyway, she thinks that made Brenda mad."

Smiling, he lays bacon in the skillet. He's fixing the only dinner he knows how to fix— breakfast. "Yeah, that sounds a little fishy," he says.

"Then, before that, she tells me how lazy Darnell is, and in the next sentence she says he takes his mom for a walk every day?"

"Does that make sense to you?"

"No. But you had to be there. It was nothing big, just some little inconsistencies. You know how some people are."

"Sure." He gets out a mixing bowl so I know we're going to have his famous omelets. "How's her mom compared to yours?"

"I didn't hear any horror stories, but I asked her where she lived and she says, 'In town, not too far.' It was hard to pin her down."

He sets the eggs down and looks at me. "If I didn't know you better, I'd think you were a bit suspicious of Ms. Mullins."

"Not really." But there is something, I just don't know what. Plus, I don't want to over-analyze a person on the second meeting just because I didn't get all the answers I wanted in exactly the way I wanted them. Maybe she didn't find out what she wanted either. More than likely, she didn't want to find out anything anyway.

"Oh, but get this," I tell him. "She must have some say-so about her mom's money or will or estate or something because she says, 'Darnell's going to do his share,' talking about her mom, 'or he's not going to get a share.' Just like that. So she must have some power over him. Maybe that's why they don't get along."

"Veddy intavesting," says Theo in his sad German accent.

He pulls the Pico de Gallo sauce from the fridge. He can never remember that name so he calls it Cinco de Mayo sauce. He thinks the Mayo stands for mayonnaise. He's going to open the tub, look at it and then ask me if there's any mayonnaise in there.

"Is there any mayonnaise in this?"

"No, honey — that's fine. That's what you use."

When he gets done the omelets are the size of footballs. He eats most of the bacon, all of his omelet and half of mine. I estimate he's knocked down about four thousand calories – real heart healthy.

#

It's the next morning when Dickey calls. Miraculously, the buyers have accepted our counter of $249,000. Their agent told Dickey that they want the home inspection done as quickly as possible. Dickey's hopeful they can do it tomorrow. He says he spoke with Dad earlier this morning. "Your father said they could do the inspection any time they wanted to. He says there's nothing wrong. He wasn't elated, but he wasn't down either."

I call Theo with the good news. He's elated. Getting off the hook for three or four thousand dollars is nice too, he says.

Then I call Mom and Dad. Fortunately Dad answers. He wants me to call Sally at Beeler's Trace today. He's anxious to put down a deposit so they'll have some place to live. He doesn't know that Sally has promised me that she'll call me if either one of the units are sold.

The whole time we're talking I can hear Mom in the background fussing about the inspection. "This house is clean," she keeps repeating.

#

They did the inspection yesterday, as scheduled. It's early when Dickey calls. He reads

the inspection report to me. It's incredible how
many things they can find that aren't right. Half a
dozen electrical issues, one bad water heater,
windows painted shut, water spot on the half bath
ceiling and a couple of other things.

"So what do we do?" I ask Dickey.

"I got this faxed to me yesterday. I gave it to
a guy I know who takes care of this type of work.
He went through it at your parent's house. I don't
think they were very happy about it. Water heater's
the biggest thing. It works, but the recycle rate is
way too long. They probably never noticed it, but if
you're doing laundry and showers for four, it needs
to be replaced. It's nearly fifteen years old.
Probably has a bad dip tube. Your dad said he was
going to drain it, but Don, that's my guy, says that's
not going to solve this problem. Anyway, with a
new heater installed, he estimated everything at
$2,970."

Damn – we're back on the hook for three
thousand. I know my dad, and he believes that he
can fix every one of these problems. I'll be lucky to
get them out of there before I'm ready for a rest
home.

"I'm sorry, Sissy," says Dickey. "Do you
think your parents would be willing to pay for it?"

My gut feeling is—no friggin' way. "I'll
try," I tell him, "but I doubt it. Let me talk to them
and I'll get back to you. I won't say anything about
us paying for it. Maybe I can convince them."

"Well," says Dickey, "it's a good offer. I
didn't think it would go this high. These people

want this particular house, if you ask me. But I
don't know how far they'll go."

"Let me talk to Mom and Dad. I'll get back
to you."

#

I take a Xanax, knock down a glass of cheap
white, pour a second, sharpen my trusty sword since
Theo isn't here, ride Honda out Palm Tree Way,
fight the good fight, lose, and ride back.

I call Dickey and he tells me the buyers want
thirty-five hundred, in case three won't cover
everything. Fine, I tell him. He's coming to get our
check. Shit.

And still no mention of any twenty grand.

#

I'm getting my way, but it's taking a toll, and
I'm not talking about the money. Now I'm listening
to Mom and Dad tell me how they got their price.

"See now, Sissy," says Dad in his
braggadocio voice. "When you add the three-
thousand to the two-forty-nine you're at two-fifty-
two. So we got it, our number. Knew we would.
You and that Mexican need more patience."

He's lucky I'm in a good mood because my
idea of patience is a very slow Chinese water
torture, and I know a couple of ideal subjects.

Dad went out sometime this past week and
raided the neighborhood recycling bins. He brought
back enough newspaper to pack New York City.

So now they're packing. Careful with those
Melmac plates, you wouldn't want to hurt them.
And those delicate insulated cups. And that

Tupperware. Put more newspaper and tape around the feet of those Duncan Phyfe chairs.

But the contracts are signed. The financing is arranged. They are legally obligated to vacate these premises effective date of closing.

I'm over here for one reason and one reason only—to convince them to spend some of their loot on packers and movers. I'm not packing a damn thing. And Theo and I are certainly not going to move this junk. Other people make a bad living doing that—big husky men. And they're going to have to hire some.

Unless Brenda hauls it all away first. She's over here every other day now. They're giving her this and that, whatever won't fit into their smaller digs. Fine. She can have it. Darnell's darling truck is racking up the miles, but that's okay because he's driving her new Kia and "holding the miles down on it."

Fine. Fine. Double friggin' FINE!

I bumped in to Brenda over here the other day, foraging. She said, "You want me to ask them about the money?"

"No," I told her. "Just forget it. Maybe they'll say something after the closing."

Meanwhile, Mom's moping around moaning about missing her neighbors whom she's never met. Dad's squinting and dodging her whip-like orders. I'm dancing around the mess trying to explain that if they let the movers pack everything, then the movers will guarantee that nothing gets broken, and if they do break something, they'll have to pay for it or replace it. But if they pack it, the movers won't guarantee anything. It's like talking to the proverbial brick wall. No amount of logic can deter these two old pack rats.

#

Theo met with Sally, the lady at Beeler's Trace. She let him go through both units to vacuum and make sure there weren't any dead bugs hanging around the carpet/baseboard interface or anywhere else. Meanwhile, I picked them up and brought them over to choose which unit they wanted. They're identical, but one of them had a better view out the back than the other one. Naturally, they took the other one. Fine. So now, instead of looking at a bunch of pine trees, they'll be looking at a steep short barren hillside capped with a dumpster. I hope that dumpster is emptied every morning at four.

#

I took a few things over a couple days ago, but they used movers to take all the big stuff. I wasn't there when they moved. It only took one day, and Brenda was over there to pilfer anyway, so she brought them over in Darnell's truck.

Mom called today griping about where the movers placed some of the furniture. I recruit the hated Theo and we come over to move stuff around. The princess of lament whines about him the whole time.

Occasionally, Theo hears her and looks at me and rolls his eyes.

In Mom's bedroom, the master, the movers have placed the furniture just like I would have. But she wants her dresser moved over by the entrance. Theo gets out his tape and measures the piece. "I don't think it's going to fit," he says. He measures the spot by the door. "Sorry, Gladys, but your dresser is too wide for that spot."

"That's where I want it," she says as though we can expand the wall space or shrink the dresser.

"It's going to cover the framing on both sides and stick out into the doorways," says Theo. "And it covers up the wall switch that controls the ceiling light and the fan. I'm sorry." He's being so nice. "Plus," he says, "It looks nice where it is."

Mom, wearing her thin blue checked housecoat over who knows what, frets over to Theo, about as close as I've seen her get to him. She pulls herself together and says, "It's my house! That's where I want it. Stan can move it later." She turns to Dad and goes into her mumble routine: "Make me move but it's still my house. My house."

Theo looks for a decision. Mom turns her old hunched body and looks over her shoulder at me as if to lay out the challenge. In that moment, I realize that the only thing missing is her broom. She wants to see what I will do. Who controls Sissy, Mom or Theo? That's what this test is all about.

I guess it has never occurred to her that maybe I control myself. I don't really give a damn where she puts her dresser. She can put it in the doorway and climb over the damn thing for all I care.

"Just move it, honey," I tell Theo and he sighs. I help him scoot it across the room. It sticks out an inch or so on both sides, its nasty crown molding protruding into the doorway on one side

and the bathroom door on the other. But that's
where she wants it.

I turn to her. "How's that?"

She nods.

"Fine," I say. "Anything else?" and they both
stand there.

"No. Done," she mumbles, and disappears
into the bathroom.

Dad acts as though a bad storm has passed.
He's relieved, even if he knows the dresser
shouldn't be there. He thanks us as we leave.

Chapter 14: No Home-Docs 4U

We're in the car making the jaunt back to our house and Theo is still laughing about the furniture deal. "I can't believe her," he keeps saying. I guess when you've decided that somebody has been dead for thirty years, and you really believe it, it may be funny to witness her pathetic attempts to demonstrate control.

But I think she's just trying to get in some more "mean" before the opportunity passes. It can't be enough to beat up Dad, day after day. But, I'm trying to get my mind around the "they died years ago" concept, despite moments like these reminding me I've still got a ways to go.

Theo, on the other hand, reached his position years ago, so he has no trouble seeing the "sad, pathetic-ness" of her "pathology," all Theo's words.

#

A midmorning low traffic transit from our house to their new condo takes about fifteen minutes. Sometimes I wonder just how far I've fallen for this drive to give me so much pleasure. I used to feel this way about upcoming trips to Europe, but now I'm reduced to taking pleasure from minimal traffic. Despite this, I'm missing my palm tree. I'll probably never see it again. Then I remember that they have burial plots out there in Harmon, so maybe I'll see it a couple more times.

I think people would be shocked if they stopped to count up the number of traffic lights they pass under, even on short excursions. I've counted, and there are a total of forty five on this trip –

twenty-four going and twenty-one coming back. But unlike before, I have choices which increase or decrease the total number per trip. It's a little bothersome though, like some of life's symmetries have been lost.

I'm trying to implement a new visitation structure. Theo the absolutist says I should limit my trips to one per week, but I don't want to spend an entire day with them. So I'm going at it a different way.

Yesterday I went to a counseling session at Home-Docs 4U. I was disappointed when I got there to find that my session was with a nurse practitioner instead of a doctor. This particular NP looked like she graduated from the Oasis Pecker Parlor; a real live nurse Goodbody. "It could be any one of us that make the call over at Beeler's," she tells me. "Either me, or Doctor Roberts, or Doctor Depanspour, depending on who's working or on call. But we certainly talk to each other and keep up on things, if that's what you're worried about."

"No," I said. "It's just that my parents present a difficult problem. They're really, well, independent would be a kind word. Stubborn and ornery would be more accurate."

Nurse Goodbody laughed. "Well, Ms. Woodson, we're used to dealing with older patients. We know they can be challenging. But they usually come around if we can build some trust. Seeing them in their homes has a calming effect, I think."

I wanted to tell her, "Whatever you do, don't steal anything. And "Don't take her clothes." And

"She lies when the truth would serve her better."
And "He forgets to take his memory medicine."
And "They don't like to pay their meager portion of
the medical bill." And "They just think all of you
are out to get their money." And "They'll damn
well do whatever they want regardless of how
senseless it is or what you say."

But I shouldn't prejudice their medical
minds. Besides, life is full of unfairness and they
deserve their share. Stan and Gladys are sure to
provide them with a healthy dose of humility.

Mom's going to run out of pills in a couple of
days so I need to get them set up with this new
group. Seems to me that doctors who make house
calls would be perfect for older people who don't
drive. But, trouble is to be expected, and I'm not
disappointed.

One thing has changed: I have to knock on
the door instead of waiting for the magical opening
I've come to dread. It takes them a few seconds to
respond during which I have a needle-like stab of
fear that maybe they've both died in their sleep.

But Dad opens the door. "Come on in," he
says in an unusually upbeat voice.

Mom is standing two or three feet behind
him. "Hi, Sissy." She turns and heads past the
kitchen, past the dining area, the open living room,
and through the opening to the glass-enclosed sun
porch.

Cheap bookshelves line the wall across from
the forty-year-old sofa. The recliner is opposite the
sliding door that goes out onto the dumpster
observation platform, aka, patio.

I sit down in the recliner. "Well, what do you think so far," I ask as they take their places on the couch.

"I met a guy," says Dad, "who was in Normandy a couple of days after we landed. He might even have been on the Texas with me. He's not sure. Nice guy, named, uh, uh, well something."

"You're kidding," I say in amazement. This is music to my ears. "Small world isn't it? Did you meet him while you were walking?"

"Oh, he's met everyone," says the beast in a scornful voice that implies he's done something wrong.

"Yeah," says Dad. "Four times around is a mile, he told me. So that's good to know. Met some other guys too."

"That's good to hear." I look at Mom. "Have you met anyone?" Since I already know the answer, this is more like an indictment, like asking Bubbles how the kids are.

"Woman next door is too loud," says her majesty, Queen Tolerance.

"Oh, Gladys," says Dad, "There's a brick wall between us. You can't hear her."

"At night I can. Yes I can, at night."

"What's she doing?" I ask, imagining that she's playing an old Valentino seventy-eight on a Philco Stereo Cabinet.

"What do you mean?"

Well it seemed simple enough. "I mean what is she doing to cause the racket?"

"Well, she's asleep. I can hear her breathing. She's a loud sleeper, her breathing."

Dad shakes his head.

These duplex patio homes are separated by a thick fire-block brick wall. Sally, the administrator, must have mentioned this a thousand times, bragging about its sound-deadening properties.

"So she snores?"

"No. She's not snoring, just breathing loud. In and out, all night long."

She says this as though it would be better for everyone if the lady next door only did this for half the night, though it would bode ill for the unfortunate woman. The books tell me to avoid this type of argument, but it would seem slightly weird to change the topic abruptly. I try a different tactic.

"Maybe you're hearing something else that sounds like breathing? Maybe it's the air conditioner or something."

"Oh, Sissy!" she says. "I know what an air conditioner sounds like. My goodness, she just breathes loud. I never." She turns her head away from me, looking out the patio doors. She sways forward and back, like she's in a rocking chair.

I decide to let it go and move on to why I'm here.

"I wanted to talk with you, both of you, about your doctors. Dad has his cardiologist, Ariswamy, and that won't change, but since Dr. McWerther has left her practice, I talked to the doctors at Home-Docs 4U. They are the ones who call on this place, usually on Fridays. They seem very nice, and I filled out all the paperwork. She said they could see both of you on Monday for a first exam. She thought it would take about an hour or so, for both of you." They look stunned. "I mean this would be so convenient. You wouldn't have to leave the house. If you want privacy, they can do the exam in the bedroom, or one of you can take a walk, or sit out by the dumpst . . .er, patio." Oops, I'm losing my touch. "So, what do you think?"

They look back and forth at each other and I can tell there's something going on here.

"Well, uh, I think your mom already has an appointment," says Dad.

"An appointment? Where? With whom?"

"I need some more pills." She doesn't want to look at me so she's left staring out those doors. She rocks nervously and swipes the tissue across her nose.

I know she's right. She has pills through Monday. "I told them that," I tell her. "That's why they're going to see you on Monday."

"Like he said," and she nods her head at Dad without looking at either of us. "I already have an appointment."

"Where?"

"At the old office — McWerther's office."

It's like a bad dream. I stand up and walk over to the patio doors. I'm right in front of her looking at the dusty hillock that leads up to the massive green box silhouetted against the skyline. I turn to her and look down. "Doctor Lane doesn't start for another month. There's no need to go back to that office."

"I like that office," says Mom, "and so does your father. So that's where we're going to go."

Thankfully, the books do have something to say about unreasonable demands. Be firm, they say. State your position, without anger, but let them know that if they choose to continue on in an unreasonable manner, that they'll have to make their own arrangements.

I back away to the center of the room just in front of the TV. Dad glances up at me, but looks down quickly. He twists uneasily on the couch. Mom maintains her stoic view of the drought-stricken hillside. The variegated grass, brown and pale green, barely clings to the rutted soil, a metaphor of the two lives in front of me.

I know finality when I hear it, and what I'm about to say will have no effect. Nevertheless, I'm compelled to try. I stare at Dad, but all I see is a picture of cowardice and facilitation. After a few calming breaths, I begin.

"I can appreciate that you like that office, but I'm sure you know that it's about fifteen minutes in the other direction from your old house. And you've moved about ten miles farther in this direction. So that means your doctor's office would be more than an hour from here. If McWerther were still there I could understand, but since she's gone it seems reasonable to find a new doctor that's closer to where you live. Do you see what I mean?"

Dad trembles, distressed. He pushes his glasses up again and again before the uncomfortable silence wins.

"Well, now wait here, Sissy," he says. "They got our files and everything over there, you know that don'tcha?"

"Oh," I say as though this is all a big misunderstanding about paperwork, something that I can easily remedy. "I'll have them send those to Home-Docs, just like the cardiologist does with your file. There's actually a business that does nothing but run medical files back and forth between doctors and hospitals."

"But the office people know us over there," says Mom.

"And we won't go that often," says Dad.

"And I suppose you think I'm going to drive you over there, separately, since you won't see the doctor together?"

They both act as if they didn't hear me. Finally, Mom says, "Brenda can take us if you can't."

"Oh, really?" I say. "I hope your appointments are on Saturdays, since Brenda works."

"At ten," says Mom. "Saturday at ten. They didn't have anything on Friday."

"And Brenda has agreed to take you to the doctor on Saturdays? Is that what you're telling me?"

"That's right." She mumbles something about money, but I don't catch it, I just know I'd hate to be someone that depended on Brenda to keep me alive.

I start through the door from the sunroom to the front of the condo.

"Now — where you going?" asks Dad.
"Sissy."

I stop, turn back. "I want both of you to know something right now. I want you to understand this as clearly as you can. Under no circumstances will I take you to that office or any other office. I don't care what happens to Brenda or to either of you, I'm not taking you from one end of the county to the other to see a doctor you've never met after I've gone to the trouble of getting you one right here in your own home. I'm leaving now, since that was the only reason I came over here. You've made other arrangements, and that's your business. I've given you the name of a cab company that specializes in taking people to their appointments, and I've met with the Home Assist people who also do it. You have their numbers if there's a problem, but I repeat, under no circumstances will I, or Theo, take you to another office. I'm going home now. If you change your mind, call me. Otherwise I'll call the home doctors and cancel the Monday appointment. Goodbye."

I march through the house, grab my purse from the counter, and I'm through the door when I hear Dad say something. But I'm not sure he was talking to me, so I continue on, close the door, and head to my car.

As soon as I hit the seat a giant shiver goes through my whole body – the kind you have when you've narrowly escaped an accident. I sit here for a few moments trying to breathe deeply and get a grip on myself. I'm also giving Dad a chance to open the door and come out here and tell me that they've changed their minds. But there's no sign of him. I start the car, back out, and leave. I even watch through the rear-view mirror, but their door never opens.

I'm longing for the Oasis, or any other sanctuary, in case I can't make it home. My teeth are chattering and I suddenly fear that my cell phone will ring and I'll have to talk to someone and my fractured state will be found out.

God help me.

Chapter 15: Brenda Wants a Favor

Theo and I talk about the doctor's office situation, and he's cheering me on. It took me a day or so to calm down, but I feel better about it. Still, the real test will come when they call me and tell me that good old' Brenda can't make it. But I'm resolved – I will not take them, Period!

Also, we have an alibi in case they call. We're going out to Sheldon's boat for the weekend.

I'm standing in the kitchen when the phone rings. It's Brenda. I take a deep breath before answering. "Hi, Brenda," I say in a cheery fashion.

"Hi, Sissy, what's going on?" She sounds like she's in a good mood.

"Not much, just trying to stay cool. How's the new car?"

"It's wonderful. I tell you, it's such a relief to have something I can depend on. You guys doing anything this weekend?"

Am I smart or what? "We're going with the Sheldon's. They're the ones with the big boat. I'm getting things ready."

"Tomorrow?" she asks. I've got to be careful here.

"Yeah, early. Too early, but I guess they've got to get some gas. Or as they say, take on fuel. He wants to get out of the marina early to beat the fuel dock crowd." It's a lie, but that should do it.

"I wonder if I can get you to do me a favor."

"What do you need?" I ask as though I'm open to helping in any way that I can.

"Well," she says in her drawn out manner, "Darnell and I are over here at the casino in Brockton. He's a member of the VIP club and they just told us that we can stay at the Honors Penthouse tonight. We saw it on a tour about a year ago. It's so incredible. It has a giant hot tub and a big bar and a round bed that's big as a whole room and it turns and it's got mirrors all around. It's really neat. Trouble is I promised Mom that I'd take her to the doctor tomorrow morning. There's no way I can make it unless we come back tonight. Her appointment's real early so I was wondering..."

"Oh, I'm sorry, but we're leaving so early, like I said."

"Well, can't you just take her early? I mean they open at like eight or something."

"Sheldon's has a departure time of eight. Sorry."

"Well, hell, Sissy, he can wait an hour, can't he?"

Now she's getting pissed. There's so many things wrong with this that I hardly know where to start. I could patiently explain everything to Bubbles like commitments, and that I know the doctor' office doesn't open until nine, and that I know it will take them thirty to sixty minutes to get her in, and that it will take another two hours to get her back home after I stop to fill her prescription, and that by the time I finish I can maybe make it to the dock by one, if everything goes perfectly. Or, I could tell her what I told them – that I wouldn't take Mom to that doctor if her life depended on it. I could go into all these things, but I'm not going to because people like Bubbles just don't get reality. Not if it interferes with their plans to gamble and fornicate on a big motorized mirrored mattress. So I don't.

"Oh, I'm sorry," I repeat, "but we promised them we'd be there, and they've made plans."

"Shit. So you're not going to do it?"

"I can't, Brenda. Tell them to call a cab. They've got a number."

"Oh, Sissy," she says.

So now I'm thinking that I'll explain everything, but it occurs to me that no matter what I say it will be grounds for an argument. Never argue with someone missing a logic circuit. "It's their problem. I warned them that they should have gone with the home doctors, the ones that come to Beeler's. I had it all set up, but they said no. And besides, it's ridiculous to drive them all the way out there to see some doctor they've never met. I'm not doing it and neither should you."

"Thanks a lot," she says. "I'll do something nice for you some day too. Are you sure?"

Now I've been threatened and challenged. The books do have something to say about that.

"I'm sorry you feel that way, but yes, I'm sure."

"Well thanks one hell-of-a-lot, Sissy. I'll talk to you later."

"Okay," I say, but she's already hung up.

#

The mongrel boy is really working Main. I point him out to Theo from our window seat at Splendito's. It's eight, but it's still too hot to sit outside. This is the next best spot, cool, but with a good view. The wind is blowing outside, but it's a hot breeze that offers no relief.

Speaking of hot, Theo's so mad at Brenda. He's calling her all kinds of names, most beginning with "That fat ..."

He has a right to be mad, but I'm more distraught about the state of my family. There are only four of us and I'm on bad terms with the other three. The only way it can get worse is if I can get pissed at myself. That's not hard to do when you look at the state of your relationships with seventy-five percent of your immediate family. I keep telling myself that my logic circuit is working and that any normal person would agree with my position. Trouble is I'm not sure how many 'normals' are out there. I wonder what mongrel boy would say?

#

It's Monday and reality is rearing its ugly head. The phone rings, right after Theo walks out of the house. We're both anxious to learn about what happened Saturday. I promised I'd call him to let him know.

Mom and Dad's new number is easy to identify, but oh-so-hard to answer. I sit on the couch and pick up. "Hello," I say in a sing-song voice. I never know which one it's going to be, but it's usually Dad.

"Hi, uh, Sissy?" he says, carefully, like he's not sure he has the right number.

"Yeah."

"Oh, uh, uh, I wasn't sure this was right, because of this new phone and everything over here." I want to tell him that I understand; it doesn't have a rotary dial, or a crank, unless you count Mom.

"It's me," I tell him. "How are you doing this morning?"

"Well, uh, I'm okay, you know that don'tcha? But your mom is not doing too well, I guess. I mean she's worried about her pills. This is her last one, you know that don'tcha?"

That damned Brenda – and right after they gave her that money. Incredible.

"Didn't she get some Saturday?" I ask anyway.

"Well, uh, that guy, uh, Brenda's friend …"

"You mean Darnell?"

"Yeah, Darnell. He had an accident, I guess. So she couldn't make it, because of that."

I'll bet he got flung off that spinning bed. Maybe lard-ass landed on him. Could have smashed into a mirror and cut his head off. I am so worried.

"A car accident?"

"Uh, yeah, I think. Anyway, she needs to get some more."

"Well, what can I do? She'll have to get another appointment with, whomever, over there. She'll have to see a doctor, I guess."

"Well, you want to talk to her?"

"I don't know what to tell her." But he's gone.

I can hear them talking, and it doesn't sound like she's too happy about having to speak with me. But I guess he can rightfully claim that he forgot that she wanted him to work this out with me. Then I begin to wonder if his memory loss has less to do with his age than trying to forget about his life with Attila the Hen. Maybe that's why he won't take his Aricept, he's afraid it will all come back.

"Sissy," she says.

"Hi. Dad said you didn't make it Saturday?"

"That Darnell guy had a wreck, so we couldn't go."

"Is he hurt?"

"I don't know. Don't know that."

"Well, did Brenda call?"

"Yes. She called. Said he'd had a wreck. Had to pick him up, or something. What's his name?"

"Darnell. Darnell something. You've met him haven't you?"

"No, we've never met him. Just used his truck."

"So you're out of pills?"

"Yeah," she says so low I can barely hear her.

"Did you call the office to get some more?"

"No. We didn't call them. It's long distance."

It's long distance by car, but not by phone. "No, Mom, it's a different area code, but it's not long distance. Besides, you can call long distance for free on the cell phone. I've told you that."

"Well, okay," she says.

Okay what, I'm wondering. "How's your shoulder?" I ask.

The first thing I hear is her sorrowful moan. "It's still hurting. Can't hardly unpack things. But we're nearly through."

"Okay," I tell her. "Give them a call and let me know what they say. Just tell them you couldn't make it." I want to add that she better not make an appointment unless she's cleared it with her limo driver, Bubbles, who's probably working today since I know that she and Darnell both took off Friday for some high-stakes R and R. Unless they're at the hospital tending to Darnell's nasty bed sore.

Instead, I say, "Have you talked to Brenda today?"

"No. She's at work I'm sure." I can barely hear the last word; it trails off into a sigh.

"Call them and let me know what they say, okay?"

"Okay. We'll call them. I'll try to find their number."

#

And I don't even feel bad about it, so I'm really making some progress in this "they died years ago," effort. But, I admit I have pressure on me from all four sides. Mom and Dad on side one, Brenda on side two, Theo on side three, and my guilty conscience on side four. But I'm determined to stick to my guns.

I need to ease them into the Home-Docs 4U system, but I have a feeling that this isn't the right time to try. So I need to get her past this problem until Saturday when Darnell should be fully recovered, allowing Nurse Brenda to earn her keep. The easy thing would be to take Mom to the old office, but that's giving in to unreasonable demands, and I'm not going to do it. Theo would be furious with me, and worse than that, I'd be furious with me.

I'm thinking about this when the phone rings. That didn't take long. But when I check the number, it's not them.

"Hello."

"Hello, Sissy?" says a woman.

"Yes."

"This is Dr. McWerther. I was calling about your mom."

"Oh, hi doc. Thank you for calling. Did they call you from your old office?"

"Yeah. I wrote a refill on your mom's Vicodin before I left, but I told the office to call me before they let it go. They said your mom called this morning."

"Are you at the hospital?"

"Yeah, Klondike on Dupree. You know, the big complex?"

"Sure, well, I'm sorry they had to bother you. Mom was supposed to get over there on Saturday, but she couldn't make it. She has one pill for today, but just so you know, I've doled them out. Nobody's taking these except her, if you know what I mean."

"Good, Sissy. Well, that's why I called. She'll have to see someone before she can get them again. I'll call them back and release the prescription. Is there a particular pharmacy you want?"

"I've got the number right here." I give her the number to the pharmacy about a block from me.

"How's her shoulder?" she asks.

"Oh she's still complaining, but you know they moved over here to Beeler's, so not too far from you. I tried and tried to get them to let the movers pack and unpack, but you know how those old people can be, and they're the worst. So she's been unpacking everything and working my dad to death. I'm not surprised her arm's still hurting."

"Okay," she says. "I'll call them back. Better check with the pharmacy. It could take them a couple hours, depending."

"That's fine," I tell her. "Thanks. I appreciate your help. I'll try to see that this doesn't happen again."

"No problem, Sissy. Good luck with them."

I could have called Mom right back, but I don't. Let her stew for a while. I give it thirty minutes and then I call the pharmacy. Another minor miracle—they have the prescription ready for pick up. I call and tell her I'll get it and bring it over. Crisis averted.

Chapter 16: Un-Hung Over Pictures

My Nirvana is short-lived. I called Theo
before I came over here. He was as incredulous as
you might expect. He's back to calling Brenda
"That fat . . ."

Dad's in an argument with Mom about the
picture he's hung on the wall in the dining area. He
centered it between the fireplace on the left and the
short wall separating the kitchen on the right. That
would be fine except the dining room table has to
set a foot and a half off-center to make room for the
eating counter, so I'm agreeing with her that the
picture should be centered over the table.

These things are exasperating because they
take so long to resolve. If it were Theo and me,
we'd choose one way or the other, and if we didn't
like it, we'd move it. But when you're dealing with
Mom, a misplaced nail hole is cause for extreme
consternation. Dad knows that he'll be hearing
about it for, well, ever.

What's worse, I don't even get a thank-you
for making the trip over here. I know she doesn't
want to talk about the missed appointment because
it involves her stubborn stupidity and her precious,
do-no-wrong, Brenda.

And, of course, there's no mention of the
twenty thousand that they gave her or that Brenda
said they would give me after the house closed. I
spend thirty minutes placating Mom about the stray
hole Dad made to miss-hang the picture. I keep
telling her that moving it over to where she wants it

has left the tiny hole covered up behind the picture. Oh, but she knows it's there.

She beats on him relentlessly until I get mad and change the subject. "Have you seen Brenda's new car? She says it's really nice."

The haranguing comes to a screeching halt. Dad's looking at her for direction. He doesn't know what to say.

"It's good." Then she mumbles something else.

"What?" I say.

"It's easier to get in than yours, I think," she says in a forceful nasty tone.

What a liar! Every time Brenda was over here she was in Darnell's truck. To the best of my knowledge they've never seen the car they paid for, so, of course, she doesn't know how it is to get into. But she's mad that I brought it up, so she insults my car. It's her way of getting back at me for mentioning it. Since I'm already upset, I decide to let her have it. "Easier than the Honda?"

"Oh." She's looking down at the floor. "Yes, I think so." She walks to the end of the table, looking back at Dad. "This is fine now, Stanley. It hides that nail hole, so it's fine."

But I am relentless. "Did you like it?" I ask Dad.

"Oh, uh, uh, …" he mumbles aloud. He hasn't a clue how to respond. It's amazing to me that people their age have forgotten the old adage, *Oh! What a tangled web we weave, when first we practice to deceive.*

I re-focus on Mom. "I think Brenda said it's a Kia."

She walks to the wall. "I'm not sure. I don't remember." She looks back at me. "I think it looks better there, don't you?"

"Yeah, that's better, over the table like that. Well, do you remember what color it was?"

"What?" She turns back to the picture. She taps one corner then the other, anything to keep from looking back at me.

I walk over and stand beside her. I straighten the picture and look down at her. "Brenda's new car; what color was it?"

"Oh." She rubs her hands together furiously. If they were made of wood they'd burst into flames. She looks at Dad, but when they make eye contact he looks to the floor.

I circle around the table. Her eyes follow me, peaking out above her glasses. "Well," I say, "surely you remember the color. I don't know much about cars, but I can usually tell the color."

To call the reigning silence a pregnant moment is to devalue motherhood. They're in a fix about a stupid lie and about the money that's caused them to lie in the first place. Now, I'm thinking that the best way to get my point across even more forcefully is to bring up that matter of how Brenda could afford such a nice new un-colored vehicle— and one so easy to get into.

"So, how'd it ride, nice?" I could hear a pin drop on the carpet. It's a toss-up to see who's going to break first. Dad's boring an eye-hole in the floor, and Mom's going to break a couple of fingers if she's not careful.

This may seem cruel, and maybe it is, but they deserve it. They've already told me that they were going to "help her out." And Dad has said, "It's only fair to give you the same amount." So I think it's only fair to make them squirm like vermin. Cheap liars, and she didn't even say thank you for the prescription.

I'm standing here looking at them, waiting. It'd take a fifty-inch chain saw to cut the tension.

I'm about to continue with something along the lines of, "so you don't know what it is, you don't know how it rides, you don't know what color it is, you only know that it's easier to get into than mine. Is that right?" But at the last second I change my mind. The books have told me to take a different tact than normal when dealing with their situation. My normal inclination would be to pursue this to the bitter end and force them to admit that they haven't seen her car. But it doesn't matter—it's just Mom. And Dad is her great facilitator. So they can stew.

Without a word, I walk past them, past the fancy sofa and through the doorway to the enclosed sunroom. I sit down on the couch across from the snap-together bookcases decorated with books, family pictures and odds and ends.

I see why they like this couch: from here you can see straight through the door, across the living and dining areas to the kitchen window. I can see them now, frozen into place. I've had some effect on Mom; otherwise, she'd follow me around to make sure I don't touch anything. But she's just standing like a statue. Dad's looking down at the floor.

I turn my attention back to the bookshelves. I begin to see a pattern in the pictures, oldest at the bottom and latest at the top. But something's not right. I look again, telling myself who's in each picture. And then it hits me: there's not a single picture of T2 or Brian or Theo in the entire set. There are two pictures of me, but mostly it's Brenda, Billy, David and Bobby. Not one picture of my kids.

So I count them. Thirty pictures in all, none bigger than eight inches, and everything framed.

I close my eyes and try to imagine the rest of their condo. Maybe they've got my family somewhere else? The only room I can't remember is Dad's. If they're not in there, then they're in a box in the garage. I stand and my legs are shaky. I'm breathing quick and shallow. I feel a little dizzy, but I pull myself together and walk through the door, past Mom and into Dad's bedroom. I stand at the foot his bed and do a three-sixty. Nothing. A window and his headboard take up one wall. Another wall has the bedroom door and a door to the half-bath. Between the two is an armoire that nearly reaches the ceiling. The third wall has a chest of drawers below a framed picture of a battleship older than I am. And the fourth wall has the set of fake cast-iron minstrel players.

My mouth is quivering. I walk back to the sunroom and plop down on the couch, staring again at the bookshelves. Not a single picture of my family, and no room left to put any.

As I look at the bookshelves and listen to the silence, blackness starts to close in. It stops before it cuts my sight off completely, leaving me with tunnel vision. No matter where I look, I see a picture of David when he was about three. And there's Bobby at maybe six on Billy's shoulders. Brenda standing behind both kids in their baseball uniforms. Then the whole group laughing, over at our house. I recognize the upright piano that we keep moving with us.

I count seven pictures of Billy. In three of them he's alone. He's been gone fifteen years and they hated him when he left Brenda, yet here he is?

I can feel my chest heaving, and I'm having trouble getting enough air. My head feels light and the TV is the shape of a pyramid.

I'm having trouble sitting up. All I can think about are the pictures I've given them over the years. I know they number in the hundreds.

My vision has narrowed even further and it's like I'm looking up from the bottom of a fuzzy well. Then I notice the frames. She's put their pictures in frames … Those are my frames! They had my kids in them! She's probably cut their pictures up into little bitty pieces and thrown them away. She's cut them up and thrown them out of here and out of her life.

I hear a noise, a piercing electric-like noise. I try to cover my ears but my arms aren't working too well, and I just can't reach them.

I'm falling deeper into the well until it's nothing but blackness.

I can feel the worn material of the sofa and realize that I need to lie down and rest, but it's too dark. Anything could be coming at me, and with the electric noise, I'd never know. I marvel at the totality of the darkness. I lie down and try to concentrate on some old memory of light and then a tiny spec appears.

It grows as it moves toward me. Somehow it's getting clearer and bigger without getting closer. It tries to come into focus, but I think it's too late because I want to sleep. I watch it for a few more seconds until it can transform itself into something recognizable.

Then, two beautiful palm trees form perfectly in my eyes. They're covered in Christmas lights, and they sway gently, as if encouraging me to rest.

I acknowledge their permission and drift off.

Chapter 17: Unglued at Home

"Sissy. Sissy! Your purse is ringing. Honey, it's ringing in there."

Can't you see I'm sleeping here?

"Sissy, it's your phone. It's ringing in your purse."

That does it. As soon as I wake up I'm going to brain somebody.

"Sissy!"

"What!"

"Honey, your phone is going off. In your purse."

"What?"

"You went to sleep. You do too much. You need more rest. Tell him to slow down."

"Who?"

But she doesn't answer. Instead she says that she made some coffee, do I want some. I didn't before she woke me up, but I guess I do now.

I prop myself up and look through a doorway to a distant window. I know this place. I recognize the back of that frilly sofa. It's Mom and Dad's formal sofa. I glance to my left and Mom and Dad are standing there looking down at me. I move to face the wall of cheap bookshelves. The pictures! Now I remember. I blink and rub my eyes. "What time is it?"

"It's nearly ten," says Dad.

Ten. I didn't get here until past nine, so I haven't been out long. God, it feels like, I don't know. If someone told me it was ten at night I'd believe them, except it's light outside.

I want to stand. I'm worried I might not make it, but my head seems clear now, not like before. They think I fell asleep. "Tell him to slow down," is what she said. She was talking about Theo, that it's his fault I fell asleep. He pushes me too hard. I ought to tell her that that's a bunch of crap, but I don't want to talk to her.

"Would you bring me my purse?" I ask. "And I'll have that coffee."

Dad mumbles something and leaves. Mom shuffles away behind him. As soon as they are out of view, I stand up. I feel okay, but tired. A few seconds later Dad hands me my purse and I dig out my phone. It's an ad, a text message. I'm still looking at the screen when she returns.

"I made you a cup. It's on the counter."

That's right, no eating or drinking outside of the kitchen. It's not an eat-in, so you have to stand at the overhanging counter that separates it from the dining area. Maybe that's where they intend to put my family – under the overhanging counter. If they ever buy some stools, people will just have to be careful not to kick my family. I drop the phone in my purse and look up.

"I've got to go. Brian needs a book at the house, and he left his key there the other day." I look at my watch. "I should be able to beat him." I can't see my face, but I think it must be pasty white. If I don't get out of here I'm going to throw up. I've got to get some fresh air.

They're talking to me as I snatch my purse from the couch, but I'm not listening. I pause at the door, pull it open, and look back. They've still got to cross the hallway beside the kitchen to get to me. I say nothing. I step onto the porch pulling the door closed behind me.

As I'm getting into my car, their door opens. Dad is saying something, but it's as if we don't speak the same language. I start the car. Now both of them are on the small porch, and Mom is saying something. I back out and drive away.

The trip home takes between twenty minutes and four hours. When I get there, I go to the bedroom, collapse on the bed, and fall immediately to sleep.

#

When I wake up, I look at the clock and it's nearly two. I go downstairs, cut off three pieces of Stilton cheese, grab a handful of Triscuits, and pour a small glass of white. Walking into the living room, I sit in the big wingback chair with the side table covered in magazines. I pick the one on top, *American Bungalow*, and flip through it. I nibble at the cheese, but give up on the crumbly Triscuits. The wine goes down good and I have a fleeting thought about getting plastered.

I'm still in a daze. I know I blacked out. I also know why. I'm not concerned about my physical health, but my mental state is certainly questionable. I should have done what Theo would have—raised hell. But that's not my way.

I'm sitting here thinking about it when I look up and see our black mahogany standing grand piano, the same one that was in the picture at Mom's. Our relationship seems to come crashing down on me and I burst into another bawling fit like the one I had at the Oasis. I can't control it, and I keep thinking how lucky it is I'm here in my own home with no witnesses.

Then: "Sissy!" It's Theo. "Sissy, honey, what's wrong?" He's rubbing my back as I look up. "What's wrong honey? Come here." He helps me stand and walks me to the sofa. We sit down. He hugs me and caresses my head as I burrow into him. "It's okay," he keeps saying. "It's all right now. It's all right."

I don't have a husband — I have a great big life preserver with legs. He needs to be orange. And rounder. He needs to be a sponge to soak up all this. But I can't stop crying. It's too painful to be excommunicated by your parents —people that you're always helping.

I straighten up, but I'm still crying and that piano is still there. Theo is trying to calm me down, but I'm in no shape to listen.

It's not right. It's not fair. Mistreat me, okay. Mistreat Theo, okay. But God damn it, don't mistreat my kids. They've always been good to you. They've respected you even when you didn't deserve it. At ten years old my kids were twice the human beings that you two have ever been. How dare you!

"The low-life sons-of-bitches," I'm screaming while Theo keeps saying "It's all right. It's all right now." He tries to hand me his handkerchief.

"I've had it! They either put those pictures up or I'll kill both of them!" I doubt that Theo knows what I'm saying because I'm crying and screaming the whole time. "And I want my frames back. Every fucking one. I want them back. And I'm going to court and I'm going to take over their whole worthless lives and they'll do what I say or they'll go to fucking jail. They'll go to hell! I swear to God!"

"It's all right Sissy, all right to be upset. It's all right. Let's talk about it," he's saying.

But I'm panting and crying and screaming and I'm so mad I don't know what to do next. "If they go to heaven then I want hell! I won't go to heaven if they're up there. You hear me God? Do you hear me? If you're taking them in, then I don't want any part of it! You can have them."

I pull away from Theo and stand up. I look at that piano. I'm huffing and crying and stomping and cussing. And I'm going to kill that piano. It's a traitor—traitor to my family! I spot a vase. I reach down and grab it. I rear back and Theo takes it away from me. He won't let me kill it. What's wrong with him?

He holds me so tight I can't move. His arms are around me and he sways me back and forth, almost singing in my ear. He's rhythmical and warm and safe, wonderful and maddening at the same time.

I need to sit down. He helps me back to the couch. He sits down with me and I sob and cry until his shirt is wet and warm. I bury my face and take shuddering breaths, wondering if I'll ever stop. Eventually, I fall asleep.

When I wake, I'm on the couch with a small blanket over me. My stomach is sore, the muscles tight.

"Hey there," says Theo. He's sitting in the wingback chair looking at me. "How're we doing now?"

"Better, I think." My voice is muffled and creaky. I start to move and he comes over to help me to sit up.

"You okay?" he asks.

"I think so. I don't know."

"Want me to call somebody? Maybe someone who can see you today? I'm sure someone is available for, well …"

"Emergencies?" I finish while trying to muster up a sad smile.

"I don't know," he says. "Is that what this is, a mad fit? What do you think?"

"I'm not sure either. I'm not sure whether I need to see someone, or see someone now, or see someone at all, or what. I'm not sure."

"You kept saying "frames". Did something happen over there?" He looks at me very seriously while holding out his hanky.

I take it and wipe my eyes. "Yeah … yeah something happened, but not enough to cause this. It's me. I've got some kind of problem." I point to my head. "Here."

"You've got two problems here." He points to his head, "they're named Stan and Gladys. Three if you count Bubbles," and he smiles.

"Brenda," I say, and I smile back.

"Vell. Zat's baetter. You haven't lost your connective tissue yet. Now, do you want to talk about it, or would you like to rest for a while. Want something to drink?"

"Some cold water, please."

He gets up and heads for the kitchen. I view that as a vote of confidence in my sanity, that he's willing to leave me unattended

I try to convince myself that I'm not the problem, but I have to admit that I am, at least partially. Or maybe it would be better to say I'm like a chemical that's stable until mixed with some other chemical, like a binary bomb. Mom and Dad are the other chemical.

If that's true, then there might be others out there with the same chemical composition as Stan and Gladys. If I should happen to bump into them – BOOM! We all go up in a fireball.

Theo's been gone for a couple of minutes. Then I hear him walking back toward me on our squeaky old floors. He rounds the doorway carrying a tray. It's got my water and a bottle of wine in a wet terra cotta cooler.

He sets the tray down. "You want something to eat?" That's just like Theo. He could survive a Grizzly attack and then say, "Boy, I'm hungry!"

"No, thanks." I pick up my glass and take a drink.

"I'm thinking," he says. "Maybe you shouldn't be alone with them anymore. You guys don't play well together."

"Suits me." The water is so good. I know he's trying to defuse the situation. I also know that

I need to come clean and tell him what happened.
It's funny. I know he'll be supportive, but I'm not
sure how.

"Okay." I take another drink of water.
"Well, I need to tell you what happened . . ." and I
go through the whole thing. I describe the blackout
as best I can, finishing with, ". . .so I drove off.
They were standing on the porch. Then, when I got
home . . ." and I take him right up to where he came
in. I finish with, "So, how was your day?"

"Better than yours," says Theo. "Much
better." He pulls a bottle of white from the cooler
and pours himself a glass. He takes a piece of
Stilton and lays it on a cracker. "I tell you, I don't
know about them. That's cruel. I mean really, just
cruel. You'd almost have to say it was on
purpose." He stops long enough to take a bite. "On
the other hand, they haven't been there very long.
So, I don't know. Maybe they haven't found your
box of pictures yet. But the frames, that's another
matter."

"It's been nearly two weeks," I tell him.
"They found all the others."

He finishes one cheese and Triscuit, builds
another. He definitely thinks better when his mouth
is full.

"Can I have some more water?"

"Sure," he springs up, takes my glass, fills it
and hands it back. "But our pictures were framed
nice." He brushes the crumbs from his hands and
chuckles. "I still remember that wedding picture of
Brenda and Chester in that frame made of red and
white hearts like the ones in Valentine candy – it

was so ugly. So maybe she did rob some of ours to, you know, spruce up David and Bobby, and the rest of them. I'm just saying it's possible. Sure you don't want some wine?"

"No, but thank you."

"So, if I had to guess, I'd say you were right, but it doesn't even matter because the whole picture thing was just the straw. They've been working on you for four damn years. And for at least three years they've had contact with one person—you. Prisoners in solitary have more interaction than that. So they're pretty screwed up."

"Well, what about me? You talk about screwed up!"

He swirls his wine around, then downs it. "I'll tell you what you do. You call my mom. Ask her about the forty-one magnum and the bathtub. Or ask her about the kitchen plates and the new boat. And I can think of a few more. Throwing a fit doesn't rank very high on my list."

Theo knows I'm not going to call Sylvia because I already know those stories. But he does have a point — they had some knock-down drag-outs over at his house — and some drunken brawls, too! But they're still chugging along and having a good time, mostly. And Sylvia was on some medicines a couple of times and Christy, Theo's sister, is on them now. So maybe my case isn't that unusual. Still . . .

"I'd like to wait," I tell him.

"Wait? What do you mean?"

"I mean wait to see if I should see a therapist or something. I'd just like to give myself some time. I guess it's my own pride, you know, wanting to work through it without turning it into a New York drama complete with a Freudian shrink. What do you think?"

"Sure." He smiles. "It's your call. I just want you to feel like you have that option if you need it. That's all."

#

We decide to go out for dinner, so we take a walk to an old favorite. The temperature is slightly bearable and we get to Ben's Den early enough to grab a shady table. We have a nice meal and there's no mongrel boy. I'll bet he's off tonight. I wonder if he's dealing with family issue

Chapter 18: Theo's Visit

They've called twice this morning, and the phone is ringing again. I'm not answering. To hell with them. They're not nice people no matter what Theo says about "maybe" and "possibly." .

We talked last night about what I'm going to tell Brenda. They'll call her if they can't reach me. I'm undecided, although it would be nice to confide in a sibling. But Brenda's not reliable, and that's being charitable. Plus, she's mad at me for Saturday, which is ridiculous, so maybe she won't call. Things can work out for the best.

Theo thinks I should take it easy today. This house hasn't been vacuumed in three weeks, so that's my plan — therapeutic house cleaning, like Mom ironing after an argument. I'm actually looking forward to it. I think I see why she liked it, and that scares me. But it needs to be done.

I'm standing in the kitchen when I hear the front door. It's only eleven, but it must be Theo.

"I'm home." he shouts into the house.

I walk out to the entrance hall. "I want a job like yours," I tell him.

"No," he says, "you wanted kids. But they're desperate for chemical engineers everywhere I look, so it's not too late." He puts his satchel on the table and gives me a kiss. "Come on in the kitchen. I need to tell you something."

I follow him into the kitchen, and he pours himself the last cup of coffee in the carafe and warms it up in the microwave. "Sit down," he says. "This is good."

"I'm all ears."

He takes a deep breath, and I know immediately that "this is good" doesn't mean really good.

He smiles to ease into it. "I went to see your parents this morning. I did something else before I went: I took a Xanax. I have to say it helped. Otherwise, I might have killed them. But I didn't because I knew how important it was for you to do it yourself."

Oh my God, I'm thinking, they must have been shocked out of their gourds to look up and see Mountain Man minus me.

"And?" I say.

"Well," and he drops his head and smiles, sly-like. "First, I think you were right about the pictures. I mean, I think they figured it out, even though you didn't say anything. The entire left bookshelf is covered in us – me, you, and especially T2 and Brian. So they had to do that yesterday. The open box was still sitting on the floor with a bunch of pictures in it."

"What did you say?"

"Well, I hadn't called them or anything, so the first thing they knew I was standing at the door. I go in and your dad is looking outside to see where you are, and your mom is giving me that scared animal look like she thinks it may be over for both of them, so that part was good. I like to start from a position of strength. She says, 'Where's Sissy?' and I tell her I'm alone. She flinched and hunched down and your dad came up behind me. 'What's wrong?' he wanted to know."

"So I just looked at them and said, 'You two are unbelievable. You're really something,' and I walk straight through the house to the sunroom and I see the picture work in progress. So I walk back in and they're by the dining room table and I say, 'so, you figured it out,' and here's the good part. Your mom says, 'We were going to put them up. Yes, we were. Tell him Stanley. Yes, we were.'"

"And your dad's doing his 'uh, uh,' routine. 'Put what up?' I said. And your mom says, 'Those pictures.' and then it must have dawned on her that I hadn't said a word about pictures. And she's like, 'Uh, oh,' like I caught her in something, which I did. So I sit down at the head of the table, under that picture she was so pissed about, and I say, 'Sit down,' and both of them grabbed a chair as far away as they could, but they sat down and they look like criminals waiting for their punishment. So that's what I did; I punished them. I told them just about everything I could think of. From lying about Brenda's car, to the twenty thousand dollars, to the medicines they won't take, to lying to the doctors, and about a dozen other things."

The whole time he's talking I'm thinking about how I feel about it. But I'm smiling. I'm not sure I should be, but I'm grinning like a monkey in a banana tree. I'm glad he went. It's like — at least somebody has rattled their cage. "Go on," I say.

"It gets better," says Theo. "And I'm glad I took that Xanax. I never even raised my voice except when I told them to sit down. So now I lead the jackasses to the water. I get on them about making you fight and fight to get them to sell the house and then fighting over the price and the repairs, and then your dad gets all puffed up, and he says, 'Now you wait one minute. If we'd have done what you wanted we'd have lost money, you know that don'tcha? We priced it too low. Way too low. You know that don'tcha?'"

"So I say, 'okay Stanley, so you got screwed on the price. Is that right?' But, of course, he doesn't want to admit that, so he says, 'No. But we had to make you all let us stand on our price. And we got it, you know that don'tcha?' And I say, 'no you didn't Stanley. That couple was through with you. They were walking out on that deal. Their agent told Dickey that they were done with it. They were looking at the other houses in there. That's why it took them two extra days to respond. And do you know why they took the deal? Do you know why Stanley? I'll tell you why. They took the deal because Sissy and I gave them three-thousand five hundred dollars.' And you should have seen the look on their faces. 'What?' says your dad. And I say, 'That's right. We covered that repair bill so the deal would go through. They were already paying a premium for a house with a thirty year old kitchen and twenty year old floors. So we knew it was a good deal. But more than that, it was worth it to get you over here so Sissy wouldn't have to drive across the county every time she turned around. So you got your price and we paid for it. So how's that?"

"So you told them?" I ask.

"Damn straight. This is a war. And I'm not even worried about it. They'll supply us with plenty more ammunition because they can't help it. But they were stunned. They just sat there, and you could tell they were speechless. And you know what your mom says? She says, 'Do you want some water?' and I stand up and they both jerk like I'm going to hit them. And I say, 'No. I don't want any water, Gladys. I want to get out of here. But I'm going to tell both of you something before I leave. I've travelled around the world to find somebody that likes you, but I can't find a single soul. Not one. Not one person on this entire planet likes either one of you. You're petty, vindictive, cheap, cruel, disagreeable, and a couple of goddamned liars. There's only one person who'd piss on you if you were on fire and that's Sissy. And you've done everything in your power to run her off. And this deal with the pictures may have done the trick. That'll be up to her. So, good luck with that. And, by the way,' I told them, 'she's not taking you, either one of you, to a new doctor. You'll either use this doctor that makes house calls or you'll find your own way. There's not a single good reason not to use them, except so you can terrorize Sissy. That's the real reason."

The more I watch him the more I'm glad he took that Xanax. He's marching around the kitchen like the Fuehrer on a stage. He's flinging his hands around and punctuating every word with a tomahawk chop or a raised fist.

"So, did you leave?"

"I was trying to, but your mom, that noble spirit, starts talking about Jesus. I'm like, What? 'Oh I don't have to listen to you,' she says. 'I listen to Jesus. He tells me what to do. That's my savior, Jesus. I don't have to listen to you because I listen to the Lord. He tells me what to do, not you or Sissy or Stanley. Jesus.'

"And your dad's looking at her like, 'why didn't I think of that?' So I said, 'Oh that's a good argument Gladys. That's the same argument used by the most evil people this world has ever known. And it's nothing but a lie. Jesus would never tell you to act like this. Never. And you're not too far from finding that out, up close and personal. You're going to be the most surprised person in the entire universe when that day arrives. But you've earned it. Goodbye.' and I left. So I doubt if it did any good, but I feel better." He sits down.

"Wow. Okay, so what do you think?"

"Nothing. Not really. I don't think it will have any effect on them. You can't talk a leopard out of its spots, but it helps you to try. I see how they are, Sissy. It's not you. For what it's worth, it's not you. And I'll tell you another thing; Brenda can go straight to hell with them as far as I care. She's nothing but a doped-up bum."

He gets up and comes around the little island. He puts his arms around me and gives me a kiss. "But," he says, "I'll support you. Whatever you do, I'm with you. You know that. I know we're not the same. We don't do things the same way, so I'll support you whatever you decide – however you want to handle them. That part's up to you. I guess

I just felt like I needed to do something, even if it was wrong. So now, what's for lunch?"

Chapter 19: Therapy Calls

What do you know? Theo actually has to go back to work this afternoon. I'm back to thinking about vacuuming this monster of a house, but our talk has put me out of the mood. I'm wrestling with the idea of getting an appointment with a psychiatrist. My gut instinct is that I don't really need it, and it probably won't do any good. But then I think that's exactly what Mom would say, and it pushes me to do it. Like Theo said the other day, it couldn't hurt.

I reach a compromise position; I'll call Dr. Bailey, my internist, and get his opinion. He'll probably have to give me a referral anyway. I talk to some woman in his office, Cheri I think, but I don't know her. He's off today, so I'll have to wait until tomorrow when he gets back in.

Ali called and we talked for a good while. She's taken over as chairwoman of the 'Find a Cure for Breast Cancer' Committee. I was chairwoman of that group the time before last. I did that for five years and turned it into a full time job. It's a good cause, but there's actually a lot to do getting things organized and lining up sponsors and donors.

Ali is perfect for it. She's serious, thorough, and most importantly, connected. T2 is involved in a dozen different local organizations and between his contacts and Ali's stunning appearance, donors can't say no. She's nearly doubled the sponsorship income over the last eighteen months.

When we're through talking, I hang up and the phone is blinking. Somebody's left a message.

I check the calls log and recognize their number. This is good; it's the first time they've left a message in a long while. They hate leaving a message. It's foreign to them. They aren't sure they have the right place, then they stumble around because they're unprepared for the challenge of saying something coherent, and most of the time they haven't really left a message, they've just hung on too long and you hear them talking back and forth in the background before they hang up. So it's always exciting to listen to it.

"Uh, hello, uh, Sissy. Uh, this is your dad, and, uh, give, give us a call, uh. We tried Brenda, so, uh, give us a call," and then there's a long pause until I hear Mom say, "Well hang up now, Stanley. Yeah, hang up," and it clicks off.

Information can be extracted from between the "uh's." It's actually one of their more precise messages. The good news is that they desperately want to talk with me. So I've got a sledgehammer to pound them with. They're so desperate, in fact, that they've already tried to reach Brenda. She's probably sitting in her office thinking that they want her to do something, so she's not going to call them back. That's how she normally operates. There have been times when they've tried to reach her and eventually she'll call me to see what they want. So I act as her call screener.

But it's Theo's visit that has them in a panic. That just doesn't happen, so they're concerned about the possibility of losing free shuttle service and a host of other services that I provide such as: Purchasing advisor, dispute resolution counselor,

assistant decorator, medical advisor, Executive Vice
President of Bananas and Onion Pickers
International, wardrobe assistant, relocation
specialist, invoice analyzer, insurance adjustor, and
future funeral director.

I've reached the point where that last job is
starting to look interesting. Perhaps I should go
ahead and call UPS and FedEx to get quotes on
what it will cost to have the bodies crated up and
dropped into a hole in Harmon. It would save me
from having to run all the way out there in a rented
limo.

The phone's ringing again, but I don't
recognize the number. I'm going to get Caller ID
just like every other over-extended, repo-averse bill
dodger, or drug dealer, or self-important person, or
just anyone who can't afford it. Caller ID is like the
state lottery – the people who pay for it are the ones
who can least afford it. I don't really want to talk to
anyone right now, but I can't help it, and I pick up
on the fourth ring.

"Sissy Woodson?" says the caller, some man.

"Who's calling please?"

"This is Doctor Bailey. Is that you Sissy?"

"Oh, hi Doctor Bailey. Yeah, this is Sissy.
They told me you weren't in today," and it's
amazing they could get that wrong, but never over-
estimate the office help.

"I'm at the house, but I checked in and they
said you'd called. What's up?" and I suppose I
should take that last cynical remark back.

"It's not an emergency or anything, and I
don't want to take up your time, but I was going to

talk with you about maybe seeing a psychiatrist. I had a run-in with my parents yesterday, and I guess I blacked out for a while, maybe fifteen minutes, on their couch. So I'm trying to decide if I should see somebody about it."

"Has this happened before?"

"No. But, I mean I know what triggered it. At least I think I know."

We spend the next several minutes going through all the questions that he must ask covering nausea, dizziness, family history, alcohol, etc.

"It sounds like it's a panic attack. Sometimes our amygdala over-responds and it induces a fight-or-flight response. One way to get out of a situation is to shut down, and perhaps that's what you did. But we don't want to take any chances – low blood pressure could be more serious. So I want you to go into the office right now and they can do an ECG, just to make sure your heart is okay. It's probably fine, but we need to make sure of that first.

"As to whether or not you need a psychiatrist, that's harder to tell. If you think you should, then you probably should, but I see patients nearly every day that I feel need some help coping with their problems. They're not being reasonable, or they have some serious addiction, and it's easy to recommend that they get some help. But we've talked about your situation before. I've told you that I'm dealing with some similar problems. It sounds like you and your husband can talk these things through, and I would agree with him that you need to have a more formal arrangement with your parents that limits the exposure. We have a tendency to err on the side of safety so it causes us to recommend one thing or another, so we're a little hesitant to say, 'No, you don't need any help.'

I feel bad about him taking all this time with me. I've offered to schedule something with him, but he seems okay with this. He's never in a hurry. I tell him that I'm "leaning against," seeing somebody.

"Okay," he says, "Well, I know several that I could recommend. Doctor Selvey is, I've heard, very good. She'd be my first choice for something like this where the problem isn't an addiction but stems from personal relationship issues. Why don't you talk about it? If you decide to, give me a call and I'll see about getting you in there. I'm going to call the office when we're through. You should get that ECG as soon as possible. If there's a problem, they'll let me know."

It's amazing to me how many things are related to the heart. No matter what symptom you've got, it could be related to the heart and they want that checked out ASAP. So I run over there, but the girl who reads the squiggly lines tells me it looks perfectly normal to her, and that my blood pressure is fine. So, I guess that's a relief. I get back home and the message light is blinking again.

This time I do recognize the number and it's Brenda. So they must have reached her. I don't want to talk with her either, and it pisses me off that she's trying to reach me. I decide that I'm not going to call her back. If she can act like a jackass, so can I.

You probably know someone like Brenda. You don't call them often, so when you do you kind of expect them to call you back since it's not like 'hey, I just called to chat.' And they will call you back, whenever they damn well feel like it. Usually it's a day or two or even three or four. At least that's how it is with Brenda. And she always says, "Oh, sorry, I forgot," or "I've been meaning to get back to you, sorry," like you are easily forgotten and put at the bottom of the list below all the drug dealers and cowboys and that giant social circle that she runs in.

I'm surprised that she hasn't called my cell phone and as I'm listening to her message, "Hi, it's Brenda. Give me a call please," my cell starts ringing and it's her again. When she wants to talk with you, it must occur immediately, but when you want to talk with her, it's whenever she has time and inclination. So I'm into the 'screw her' mode and I just let it ring. Whenever I talk to her, she better start with an apology about last Saturday or I'm going to hang up on her.

I know that this anger I have for all three of them isn't good for my mental health, but I can't shake it. I'm going to take some time off — a week or so.

I call Theo and update him on my talk with Bailey and about my ECG results. But I really called to let him know that I'm not available for any of them. He's in complete agreement.

#

It's been two days and I've had four messages from the trio, but I'm holding fast. I know all of

Brenda's numbers – home, work and cell. So she does the obvious thing and calls me from an unknown number.

"Oh, hey Sissy. I've been trying to reach you."

I'm in no mood to play nice. "I know that, Brenda."

"What's wrong?" she asks innocently.

"Nothing's wrong. What do you want?" and I'm harsh.

"Well, it sounds like something's wrong."

"What did you want?"

"I just wanted to talk to you, see how you were doing." Oh sure. She's always checking on my wellbeing.

"I'm fine, thanks."

"I just wanted to see."

"So now you know. I'm fine."

"Mom says she hasn't talked to you for three days. She said they left some messages."

"That's right. I'm taking some time off from those two. A week or so — whatever I want." I should add that she can go ahead and apologize, but she probably doesn't have a thought about it.

"Oh," she says. "Is something wrong?"

"Nothing that a good break won't fix," and I want to go on, but I resist. Every time I respond I leave her in an awkward position which she wholly deserves.

"A break?" she says.

"Yeah — a break from them. Some downtime." I stop again.

"I know they can be pretty miserable," she says. What she knows is debatable, but I let it pass.

"Yes they can."

"Well, what happened? I mean something must have happened."

It's hard to tell what she actually knows. Mom and Dad are both notorious liars. But I can't believe that they didn't tell her that Theo was over there, and that's enough to say that it was something serious.

"Look, Brenda, I'm tired of fooling with them. It's been a real battle getting them to move and everything and I'm fed up. I'm going to stay away for a week or so. I don't want to talk to them; I want to be done with them for a while. I'm sick of it, okay?"

"She said she thought you were mad about some pictures that she hadn't unpacked yet. Is that it?"

So they have talked about it to her. I should have figured as much. Normally they don't pass any information between Brenda and me. It's another one of Mom's protective schemes just like with her doctor. She knows that information is power and she wants that all to herself. But she's had to reposition herself here. If I don't talk to her and do her bidding, all the knowledge in the world won't help her.

"What she should have said was some pictures she wasn't going to unpack. That's what she should have said. But that's only part of it," and then I think of something. "My doctor said it was like the straw that broke the camel's back. He recommends that I take a break. So that's what I'm doing. Was there anything else you needed?"

"Your doctor? Did you see a doctor about it?"

"Just my regular doctor. I needed a more powerful anti-anxiety drug. He suggested that I avoid them for a while to see if that won't help, so you tell them that's what I'm doing."

"When do you think you'll be back over there?" Now I'm starting to smell something. Brenda acting like she really gives a shit is way out of character unless there's something in it for her.

I sigh deeply, "I don't know, a week. Something like that. At least a week, although a month would be better. Or a year."

"So like, four more days?" she says. And there it is. I knew it. She's taking the three days past and adding it to four more to come up with seven days – one week. Four days from now is Monday. Something is going on Monday. I'd stake my life on it. Some imposition to Brenda.

"I don't have the flu. It won't be gone in four days, so I can't say when. Whenever I feel like I can handle them without going completely crazy. That's when. Okay? Do you follow me?"

"Okay," she says, and she's getting in that nasty disposition again. I swear to myself that if she says one wrong word I'm hanging up. "I guess they're worried about going to the grocery store and getting their medicines and stuff like that. That's why I was asking."

"They've got all kinds of ways to do that. I've given them a dozen different ways. You three will just have to work it out."

"They'll have to work it out," she says, quickly. "I'm on vacation next week and we're going to Memphis, so they'll have to figure it out for themselves."

"Then let them," I tell her, and I told you so. She's leaving tomorrow, you can bet on it. She's probably been hit with the bill for that new car – the strings that come attached to any nice thing they do. That's why she wants me back in the saddle again, to run their errands. I can see the whole plan.

"Well, you're going to be around aren't you, next week?"

"I wouldn't count on it. Depends on how I feel. I'm not running any errands for them though, I can tell you that. They've got one of those buttons they can push if something goes wrong, so if they start to drop dead from hunger, they can just use it. I don't give a damn if they croak over there. Does that answer your question? Anything else?"

I'll bet her vacation is on the line here. And I'll bet that they're using money left over from the car. Then I think about the car. There's an outside chance that she didn't even buy a car. Who knows? Could have paid off a gambling debt, or just gambled it away.

"Well," she says, "I'm not going to go if you feel that way. Somebody has to be around."

"That's up to you. Do whatever you want," which is what you always do anyway.

"I had to take my car into the dealership," she says. "It's got some kind of problem with a wheel bearing or something. So it'll be in for a few days."

These bums are easy to predict. But before I answer her, my mini gray matter churns out all the possibilities involved here. First of all, it shouldn't matter since the dealership would damn well give me a loner on a brand new car that had a serious problem. Or maybe the unspoken-of car wreck involving Darnell also involved her car. Who knows? But one thing I do know is that I'm not bailing her out on this.

"Sorry to hear. Brian had problems with his and borrowed the bimmer, otherwise you could use it. These cars are something." That's some shrewd, on-the-fly, lying. It must run in my family.

"Oh," she says.

"Listen, I better get off here. Theo was going to call about dinner tonight. If you talk to them, tell them I'm fine and to quit calling me. I'll call them in a week or so, whatever. Okay?"

"You sure?"

"Of course I'm sure. Goodbye," and I hang up. That's for not apologizing for the last time you acted like an ass and hung up on me. I'm going to start defending myself against the whole damned trio. It's my mental health that's in jeopardy. They've already lost theirs.

Chapter 20: Insuring a Marriage

It's been a week, and I haven't had a Xanax for four days. I have had some wine – red, the good stuff. Somehow, if the bottle costs more than twenty-five dollars, it's not a crutch, it's an oenological expedition. Theo tells me that he's noticed a difference in my demeanor.

Dr. Bailey called this morning to check on me and to ask if I'd thought about Dr. Selvey, the shrink. Of course, he doesn't call her that. Apparently, she has an opening Monday at one, if I'd like to see her. I'm still undecided about it, but I also know that I'll have to see them eventually, and who knows, maybe I'll be in the psychiatric ward afterwards. With that possibility in mind, and the difficulty getting an appointment with her, I agree.

As soon as I hang up, I wish I hadn't agreed to the appointment. I suppose that I'm old enough to remember when it was viewed as slightly shameful to have to see a doctor about a psychological issue. But more than that, I'm really going because I know Mom wouldn't. That's not a good reason. Once again I'm caught in this land of indecision. Who knows, maybe she can help me with that?

It's been a good week. I managed to get the place half-way cleaned up. Ali and T2 were over last night, and we had a delicious meal. They started talking about backing me in a new restaurant. Not seriously of course. I told them that if I handled bad customers the way I handle Mom and Dad, we'd have to name the place Sissy's House of Fits and

Grits. That got us laughing about all the potential
names for restaurants and dishes that exploited my
situation: Crying Crepes, Bawling Bisque, Fish and
Fits, Psycho Salad, Gotta Beef Jerky, etc. So you
can see that I'm a good sport.

Ali and T2 think I'm crazy to see a therapist.
I know that sounds funny, but that's what they said.
At first I thought they were just being kind, like, 'oh
it's nothing,' but after a while I got the distinct
impression that they were serious. They've heard
all about my troubles, and apparently they think
blacking out and trying to kill a piano with a vase
are perfectly normal reactions.

After they leave, Theo and I have a long talk
about when, or if, I should reconnect with my
family. He thinks I should take at least another
week off. I think I've got my point across, and I
also have to admit that maybe they did plan on
putting up those pictures. Who knows? Well, they
do, of course.

I'm debating when to call Mom and Dad, and
I'm curious as to how they've managed. I'm sitting
on the sun porch after putting away all the dishes
from last night when I hear the door buzzer. When
I get there, I can see Brenda in the bevels. She
should have called, but I guess she'd argue that I
wouldn't answer. When I open the door, Darnell's
big red truck is out front, and once again I'm
wondering why she isn't at work. Then I remember
her vacation.

"Hi, Brenda — come on in." She has a sullen
look that matches her stooped shoulders and faded
blue sweat suit.

"Hi," she says as she pours through the giant door and heads toward the porch. "Sorry I didn't call, but I didn't know," she says. I'm not sure what she didn't know, but I grab an ashtray and follow her.

"What'll you have," I ask as she trundles through the kitchen.

"Just a Coke," she grunts.

It's easy to tell that she's not here with good news. She's dealt with them for four or five days, so I guess her distraught demeanor should be expected. That's fine. Grow up. I take the Coke out to her, and she's puffing away. Her swollen eyes make me think she's been crying. I'm prepared for the worst.

"Have you talked to Mom and Dad?" I ask.

She nods her head. "They're fine. But I've got some other news. They fired me," and she takes a deep drag and pushes the smoke out like she's angry with it.

"Oh my god! Why?" This is bad news.

"Seeing Darnell, I guess," she says and she's staring off.

"They fired you for dating Darnell?" Seems odd. I'll bet there's more to it.

"Well, they don't say that. They say something else, but that's what it is," and now she's looking at me angrily, like it's partly my fault.

"What did they say, because that's illegal I think. Isn't it?" and I'm waiting on the rest of the story.

"Oh, just anything they can come up with. Late to work. Lunch too long. Left early. Absent.

Shit like that," and she knocks the fire off the end and chases it around the ashtray. "That son-of-a-bitch Cecil hits on you, and if you don't give it up — he fires you! Bastard!"

Just so there's no confusion here, they fired her because she wouldn't fool around with Cecil and because she's dating Darnell, but they gave bogus reasons like late, absent, left early, long breaks, etc. I'm certainly not a legal expert, but I'm thinking that if everything she says is true, I'm going to own a trucking company. But I know her, and everything she is saying is not true. And I know how to find out. Let's see how fuzzy things get.

"You should see a lawyer. They specialize in that. It's not legal to fire somebody for not having sex with them. Did they give you any warning or anything?"

She's still staring off into space, and it looks like she's going to cry any minute now.

"Oh sure. Cecil's been bitching at me for a year. Prick."

"About what?"

"Just shit. He knew I had car trouble. He knew that. And I've been there twenty-five years so if he's gone, and Tonya's there, what's he care if I leave early. And sometimes it takes more than forty-five minutes to eat lunch. So every little thing becomes something, some big deal or something."

All the adults in the house can read between these lines since they're about a mile apart.

"Have you said anything to Mom and Dad?"

"Yeah, they're okay. I just told them the truth," and she starts to laugh a little. "Mom wanted to know if I wanted her to call them. I'm like, sure Mom. That'll fix everything. Like it was school or something. Dumbass." and she looks directly at me. "Those two are a pain in the ass – even a big one like mine. Anyway, I just wanted to let you know. I've got to do something. Find another job, I guess. I know all the guys around here. Really, it's fine. I was sick of that place anyway. It's insurance that bothers me. Cobra's about a million dollars a month. Like how can I afford that, and I don't even have a job? That's a big help — big damn help."

"Well, I'm sorry to hear this. Maybe there's some way they would agree to take you back. You think there's any chance?" but I know the answer. It's over. When she says that she was sick of that place anyway, it's over. She doesn't have a case, and she knows it.

"I don't even want to go back. But I wanted to tell you something else. Darnell says I can ride his policy."

I'm lost. "What do you mean?"

"We're going to get married."

"You and Darnell?"

"Well, yeah. How else am I going to get insurance? That'll teach them. They're going to carry my fat ass. They ain't going to fire Darnell for getting married. So we're going to do it. Sometime soon. Probably go away, Vegas or something."

"You better think about that," I warn her. "I mean how much is insurance? Mom and Dad could help out. You don't want to get married just for insurance do you?" and I can't believe what I'm hearing.

"Oh, we're in love. We were going to move into his place anyway. We just weren't going to get married. But now we'll have to. So I just stopped to let you know. Mom and Dad don't know about this, so don't tell them. Okay?"

It's like somebody told you they murdered someone then says, don't tell the police, okay? Why in the hell is she telling this to me anyway? I'll bet I'm about to find out.

"Are you just going to show up and say, here's my husband?"

"Yeah, that's why I'm here. You've got to get back over there Sissy. I've got a lot to do now – get married and find a job. So — a lot. I can't be screwing with them," and she's got that pleading look. "Well?" she finishes.

I know that Brenda only thinks about Brenda so I know this isn't going to work, but I try anyway.

"Wouldn't it be better to see if you can get another job first? I mean, getting married, that's a big step. You might be able to find a job before you can find a chapel. What's insurance for a couple of months? Are you sure?"

"It's not getting married Sissy. That's not the problem. It's the damn money. I mean you got Theo and all this," and she swings her arms around. "You don't know what it's like. Insurance will cost three-hundred a month. But we're okay for now. I can rob my 401 for a few thousand. So we're okay for a while. But I've got to find something in a couple of months."

"Well," and I'm confused again, "when do you plan to tell them? You have to tell them sometime, don't you?"

"You know the old saying," and she's started to perk up a little bit, "it's easier to get forgiveness than permission. So it's gonna be after the fact. Not before. They're not going to like it a damn bit anyway. So screw them. Maybe they don't have to know. I don't know. So, are you going back or what?"

We've gone from nearly crying about the disaster to she's going to take a couple months off. I'm suspicious that the whole story is concocted to get me back over there. But I doubt it. It would be easy to check it out, just call her office. So I can't really say anything.

"Yeah, I'm going back. I'll call them today. But I'm telling you this – if they act any worse, I swear to God, I'm through with them. I mean it. I can't handle them."

It looks like the sun rose in her face. "Good," she says. "That's good. Cause I'm going to need some time. Darnell and I have a lot to do. We have to see when he can get off. Maybe next week. I don't know."

Oh yeah. You'll need a week in Vegas to settle on a plan to make up that three-hundred a month. What a bunch of horse crap.

"You better think about it," and that's my last warning.

"I have thought about it. That's all I've thought about. I'll tell them. They're going to be pissed, I can tell you that. Hey," she says like she's about to ask me if I want to go with her to a barn dance that she just remembered, "do you know about their will?"

"No. They're real secretive about anything like that. Why?"

"They said they needed to make some changes or something. Said it was in town, near you. I ask them what, but they just said it was something they needed to do. Dad acted like he wasn't too happy about it. They'll probably say something to you. Ask something."

"Yeah," I say, "they'll ask me to take them to his office. Last time it took two or three trips, and they wouldn't tell me what it was about. I have no idea how they've got it set up. They damn sure aren't giving it to a charity. That would be too kind," and I laugh.

"I know this," she says, and she stands up, "I gotta go. But I know this, they're nuts. Nutty nuts. We might have to do something if they go any further downhill. Might have to."

"Oh yeah?" I say. "Well you take it up with them. I offered to get their power of attorney so I could sign stuff, and they acted like I was trying to steal their last penny, so I'm not saying anything. Mom will do whatever she wants anyway, so it won't matter what either one of us says," and we're talking as she reaches the front door.

She looks at her watch. "I gotta run," and she heads down the steps, "he's waiting," and she motions at the truck.

"You mean Darnell?" I say, shocked.

"Yeah, he had some calls to make. We'll see you. Make sure to call them, okay?"

"He could have come in," I shout.

"That's okay," she says and the passenger door creaks open before she gets there. She opens it up, climbs in and waves. "Bye," she shouts back as she closes the door, and the truck pulls away.

Back on the porch I'm considering her miraculous transformation from fired victim to vacation planner. Leave it to Brenda to turn a disaster into a week in Vegas. She isn't looking for a job for a couple of months. They need to see when Darnell can get off. I can see that they're really pressed for time.

No, she got fired all right, and she's using it to get me back over there so she is free to do whatever she wants. That's typical Brenda. I'm going to make it a point the next time she shows up to ask about the status of the vehicle she's in. Is it running? Is anyone inside? And I'm even more suspicious about the new car that no one in the family has seen. I should have asked her about it, but it didn't cross my mind. I guess I was too worried about her new unemployment status.

I look at the phone. I might as well get this over with.

Chapter 21: Dead Man's Stools

They were gooey sweet on the phone, and when I get here Mom's fixed me a bowl of ice-cream to "enjoy with them." I'm very suspicious of this treatment. It looks like an apology for misbehavior, but I'm not going to mention the last episode. I stopped on the way over and picked up a dozen things from the grocery store. It makes me wonder just how much time Brenda's spent carting them around.

"I talked to Brenda," I say, since it doesn't look like they're going to mention it.

"Oh, you did?" says Mom. She steps around Dad and me at the stand-up eating counter, and I can tell she's shaking.

"Yeah, it doesn't look too good."

"It's that guy she works for," says Mom. "He sounds like he was out to get her. Terrible. And she was so close to retirement. It's just a way to cut some costs. That's what it is."

I want to say that it's just a way to cut some fat, but I resist. Instead, I change the subject. They're not going to say anything sensible about Brenda anyway.

"How long are you two going to eat standing up at this counter? Don't you think it's about time to buy some stools? I looked before I came over, and Tilson's got a big sale going on. Why don't we run over there and get some?"

"Oh, uh, we've already got some coming," says Dad. "Some nice ones." He's wearing a big smile. I'm shocked that Brenda took them out.

"When?" I ask.

"Soon as he's dead." His words, juxtaposed against that satisfied smile, give new meaning to incongruous.

"What?"

"Soon as that guy's dead. Pretty soon."

I look at Mom as though he's gone completely crazy. The stools will be here as soon as some guy's dead? I stay fixed on her.

"His name's Bob, Stanley," and she shakes her head like that explains everything.

"Bob?" I say.

"Can't think of his last name," says dad. He looks at Mom. "Do you remember?"

"You never told me. Or you forgot." Her head pecks around to me. "His memory is getting worse every day. It's terrible. I don't even know where Bob's is, or how we're going to get them over here. He can't even describe them."

"Can too," he says, defensively. "They're some kind of iron with a yellow cushion," and he pauses, "or, uh, orange. One of those."

Welcome to the *Twilight Zone* meets *Looney Tunes*.

"Wait a minute. What do you mean 'when some guy named Bob dies?' What's that about?"

"Oh, he's close," says Dad. "And I got them cheap. Real cheap. And they're good ones too," he straightens with pride.

"We're buying them from the estate," says Mom. "From Bob's estate. But you can't do that until he dies. So that's what we're waiting on.

He's already gone longer than he was supposed to," and she focuses this accusation at Dad.

I sigh deeply. "Now wait a minute you two. Does Bob live here, at Beeler's?"

"Used to," says Dad, "right around the corner, about four or five houses. But he's gone now. He's in the hospital. His son made the deal. Supposed to be pretty nice stools. Twenty-five each. Said they cost nearly two hundred dollars apiece."

"But you can't get them until he dies, right?"

"Right," says Mom. "Thanks to your father."

I guess there's a certain logic to this after all. It's the logic that attends all misers. They'd rather eat standing up for an indefinite period of time while praying that some old guy dies so they can get a deal on his stools. Is it just me, or is that kind of morbid and really just disgusting? I don't know who the son is, but he wholly deserves to be my brother.

"What if he recovers?" I ask, not because it will make any difference, but just to see what idiotic tortured rationalizations burst forth from Mr. and Mrs. Scrooge.

"Says he won't," says Dad. "Said he was a goner. Supposed to happen last week, but I guess he's a real fighter. Got to respect him for that." He laughs. I can't imagine what that laugh is about.

"You never know, though," I say.

"We haven't paid him," says Mom. "My goodness, you must think we're crazy. We don't pay until he's dead and we get them, right Stanley?"

Dad nods. "That's right. If he lives, there's no deal."

I think I'll pray that Bob lives just to spite them. It would serve them right for him to outlive them. There would be a certain irony if we found both of them dead at the bottom of the counter. Even better if the coroner's report said they died of indigestion from unnatural eating positions. I know I shouldn't be thinking like this, but damn.

"Okay. Well I'm going to head on back."

"Well, what did Brenda say?" asks Mom.

"About what?" I'm surprised that she even wants to mention her.

"You know, don't you?" Her face lengthens, pulling her cheeks in.

"I know what?" I'm thinking that Bubbles has told them about getting married, but doesn't want me to say anything? Weird. So I'm staring at Mom.

"She was supposed to tell you," she says, "so you'd know."

"Well if she told me, I don't know what it was so why don't you tell me? How about that?"

Mom's rubbing those hands together again like whatever it is, it's mighty worrisome. Dad's looking down at the floor again in his usual default position that signifies that he's no part of this conversation. He was so happy talking about the stool steal, but now he's stooped over, watching the floor.

"We need for you to take us to that lawyer – the one who did our will. We need to make some changes. We told Brenda. She was supposed to tell you, but I guess she chickened out."

"Oh," I say, "yeah, she told me. I just didn't know what you were talking about. Do you have an appointment?"

"You're not mad?" asks Dad, as he straightens up.

"Well I hope we don't have to make three trips," I say, "but I'll take you. When?"

"I'll call you when I talk to him. But is it okay?" asks Mom.

I'm baffled by this sudden consideration.

"Sure," I say. "Just let me know."

"Right," she says, "I'll get an appointment and let you know. Maybe next week."

I nod, leaning sideways against the counter.

"She ain't right," says Dad. "Your sister ain't right. Sometimes she trips on her tongue."

"Stanley!" says Mom, defending the tongue tripper. I don't doubt that she trips. As a matter of fact, I know she does, especially around them.

"Maybe she's taking something to calm her down," I offer.

"Is not," says Mom forcefully. "She's just upset about the job thing. That's why we'll have to help her. Help her out some." More kindness on the part of these philanthropists. Amazing.

"She'll just have to find something else," I say.

"Who'd hire her?" asks Mom in the first truthful statement I've heard out of her in years. "She's too heavy, and now she's too old. People just want young people these days. Don't have to pay them as much. It's all about money to some people. That's all they care about. They don't care if it hurts somebody or not. It's just about the money."

Yeah, Mom, you've got that right. The inconsistencies between thought, word and deed around here are striking. Next thing you know they'll be talking bad about people who make deals on sick people's furniture.

"Well, let me know," I tell them, and I grab my purse.

"You think she'll be all right?" asks Dad.

"Yeah, she'll make it fine. Don't worry about Brenda. She knows all the trucking firms in town. She'll probably get a job with one of them. She seemed fine to me when I talked to her. I need to go," and I head to the door.

"Hope you're right," mumbles Dad. "I hope," he says softly.

"I'll let you know," says Mom as I leave.

#

When I get home, the blasted message light is blinking on the multi-unit phone system spread around the house. Everywhere I go, a phone is blinking away. It demands that you pick up the message immediately, if not sooner. "Answer me. Answer me!" it says in light code.

It's Carolyn. She asks if I could meet her around two at Ben's. She has some news I might find interesting. She'll be surprised to find out that I already know about the big Vegas wedding. Then I remember T2. Carolyn's going to be part of our family. I'll bet that's not good news – could be some rules about nepotism with suppliers or something. A shiver goes through me. I call Ali immediately and tell her. I hate to call T2 because I never know where he is, he travels so much. But she says he's in town, and she'll have him call me. A few minutes later the phone rings, and it's him.

"You're kidding," are the first words out of his mouth when I answer.

"Afraid not," I say, and he laughs which is a big relief to me. We have a nice chat, but he doesn't think it has anything to do with the bank and his company. He's glad I let him know because he'll talk with some guy named Phil who runs the bank just to be out front with it. But other than another stupid move by Aunt Brenda, he's fine with it. I get the impression that it's not a big deal to him.

Carolyn's message says she's away from her desk, so I tell her that I'll meet her there at two. I call Theo and get him posted on all the news. He thinks we should have a surprise party for Mr. and Mrs. Darnell on their return from Las Vegas. He's a big help.

I walk over about ten minutes early, and Carolyn is sitting outside at the shady table with a glass of wine in front of her. The place is empty.

"Hi, Sissy," she says as I sit down.

"How are you doing?"

"Good. I got our table. Thanks for coming. I know it was short notice. I hope it didn't interfere?"

"No," I say, "not at all. I was thinking about doing some more cleaning so you saved me."

The waiter takes my drink order. He remembers me because Theo acted stupid the last time we were here.

"He's so funny," he tells Carolyn. "He had us all laughing."

Theo's a regular riot. This young man waiting on us got desserts mixed up the other night, and Theo ate half of somebody else's before the kid recognized the mistake and came over to offer to get him what he ordered. Instead Theo made a big deal out of finding the guy who had his and walking over to him to offer an exchange. That guy played along and he and Theo are shouting across the restaurant at each other inviting the other sane patrons to join in on the big dessert swap.

It's just like a man to eat something he didn't order because he doesn't remember what it was. So Carolyn listens to the story from the waiter, and we're both laughing at this kid who has a future in stand-up.

"Wow," says Carolyn when he leaves, "who knew you could have so much fun at two in the afternoon? I'm going to move down here, if I can afford it."

"We love it," I say, "but there are some downsides too. Panhandlers are always around, bugging you. Don't give them anything. They just buy drugs or booze and pee on your lawn."

"Well," she says, and she moves in closer, "I told you that I had some news. I don't want to steal anyone's thunder, but if my mom's got it right, Darnell and Brenda are planning on getting married." I can tell from the look on her face that she's worried. "I hate to spoil your day," she adds.

I'm nodding my head. "They were over this morning," I tell her. "Brenda came in to cry about losing her job, then she tells me they're getting married so she'll have insurance. Is that what you heard?"

She waits until the young man sets a glass of white in front of me. "Yes. And Mom's so upset. You mean they came over this morning, because I didn't know Darnell ever got up before noon?"

"Bright and early," I say. "But Brenda had a reason. Since she's lost her job she had to get rid of Mom and Dad to be totally free to waste her time on other things like wedding plans and vacations and things like that." I'm laying it on the line.

"He's a real piece of it, if you know what I mean," she says. "He's always joking around, practical joker. I hope she knows what she's doing."

"He's the one who better watch out," I tell her. "She's one of the most selfish people I've ever known. We need to start thinking about how we're going to handle the divorce – try to stay on good terms," and we're both laughing.

We spend the next half hour talking about them and most of it isn't good. She apparently thinks Darnell isn't serious enough about life. He has four kids from two previous marriages. One of them is in jail for drugs. She keeps repeating that he's lazy, but all in all he doesn't sound too bad compared to Brenda, but maybe that's just me.

Then she tells me that she and Darnell are half-siblings; they have the same mother, but different fathers. Her dad died twenty years ago. Darnell's dad lived in a Section 8 apartment in Finley Square before dying of liver failure from drinking.

I take it all in, and it sounds like Brenda has managed to trade down a fourth time, although that isn't fair to Darnell since it would be hard to get much lower than Chester. I tell her about David and Bobby and their estranged relationship with Brenda.

We have a nice talk, and she finishes by saying, "I just wanted to make sure there were no, you know, surprises. But I guess if they told you, they're serious. Nothing against Brenda, but I'd almost be willing to chip in on the insurance if we could keep this from happening. He's just irresponsible, no drive or ambition or anything."

"I've never had any luck persuading Brenda to do anything, even when I've tried," I tell her. "I guess we should at least toast to our new extended family," and we clink our glasses.

"Oh," I say. "One thing I should tell you, not that it matters much, but Brenda hasn't told Mom and Dad. She's planning on springing it on them after the fact. That's what she said. So now I'm dealing with them without saying anything about it. That's an example of how she is."

"I know this much – my mom's not very happy about it," says Carolyn. "She's afraid Darnell won't show up to take her on her walk if he's married. She's pretty selfish too."

We've each had a glass of wine, but that's all Carolyn wants since she needs to get back to work.

I'm glad we had this talk. Carolyn seems like a nice, level-headed person. I shouldn't be surprised that my sister has a problem with her. At least I'm up to date on things that I'd probably never hear from Brenda. Once again, we promise to keep each other posted.

Chapter 22: Twisted Iron Souls

We spent the weekend on *Aquantum Leap*, Sheldon and Deidra's boat, and had a wonderful time. They're in Tampa at one of Sheldon's conferences. I'm not up on all the nautical terms, but I've learned a few; the boat's not 'parked' at the marina, it's 'docked.' And you don't go downstairs, you go below. And unless you want to party, you better stay below, because people wander over if they see you outside. Soon enough the whole back of the boat is covered with people who know Sheldon and Deidra well, call Theo "professor," and drink everything you brought plus whatever they can find in Sheldon and Deidra 's wicker liquor basket.

On Monday I met with Dr. Leonora Selvey. She had my file from Dr. Bailey, and she went over everything. She took my blood pressure and looked into my eyeballs with some contraption. Eventually she agreed with Bailey that I had probably experienced an anxiety attack, although blackouts are not common, so she advised me to avoid stressful situations with Mom and Dad as best I could. She talked to me about calming strategies, but most of them I'd already read. She also talked about the interactions of the drugs and alcohol, but she seemed to think that a more serious concern in my case was hormonal imbalance associated with emotions and post-menopausal conditions. But she didn't see anything unusual in my blood or urine assays. She talked about writing me a prescription for something, and then decided against it. The best news was that she didn't think she needed to see me again unless I had another blackout episode at which time she would order up a battery of more detailed tests. We didn't do any of the Freudian couch stuff, and I left glad that I had seen her, but none the wiser for the visit.

It's Wednesday and I'm making what I hope will be my only trip over to their place this week. There's no mention of going to the doctor, and they better not say anything about it because I'm not taking them. We go shopping which is the usual ordeal, especially when they've got a lot to buy. It's made easier because there's a Kline Bros. coffee house in the same strip mall. I bought a couple of magazines and sat inside drinking latte and looking at the pictures.

I cart in all the groceries except the two small bags Dad can manage. We pile them on the counter sans stools, and I listen to both of them gripe about Bob clinging to life. I don't say anything as we stand there eating some cheese and crackers. Mom and Dad are so bent over now that they can almost rake food off the counter directly into their mouths.

I wonder if they realize that I haven't made one trip back to the sunroom to review their new decorating scheme that supposedly includes my family. Normally, that's where we'd go to sit down, but the last time I was here I was all business and that's the way I am today.

As soon as I finish my tea I head back home.

\#

It's Friday and Mom called. They've got an appointment with their lawyer on the twenty-seventh, so a couple of weeks from now. I thought that was a long wait, but apparently he has to incorporate the changes they want and have a new document printed. I'm very tempted to ask them about it, but given my experience the last time, I decide to avoid any potentially stressful situations, as the doctor ordered.

#

No one's heard from Brenda for nearly two weeks, but I recognize the cell phone number when she calls.

"Hi, Sissy." She's all bubbly.

"Well is this the new Mrs. Darnell?" I ask.

"What? Oh. It's Davis. Darnell Davis. But yeah, this is the new Mrs. Darnell Davis-Ray. I thought it sounded more modern adding Ray. What do you think?"

I'm trying to remember what her last name was before. I can't remember Chester's last name, and I think she used that until now. Shows you how close we've been. I sit down in the living room.

"Davis-Ray – sounds like a fish," and I laugh.

"You're getting that mixed up with Devil-Ray," she tells me. Oh really? I didn't know, Bubbles. "Anyway, I told you it was Davis when we were looking at his truck. Remember, Double D, DD, on the back of his truck. Get it? Double D, Darnell Davis," and she's laughing like she's on something.

"Oh yeah," I say, but I don't remember that at all, and I think I would. I guess it's safe to say that Darnell Davis is into big boobs. He's got the mother lode now. "So how was it?" I ask.

"Hot," she says. "I mean hot hot. I think one day it got up to a hundred and fifteen. But we had a great time, indoors, if you follow me," and she laughs and laughs. I don't want to follow you there, Bubbles.

"So the marriage went all right? Did you use one of those chapels?"

"Yeah, it went great. I have some pictures. You should have seen the couple who stood up with us. They were getting married right after us so it only cost an extra twenty dollars, and they're dressed in all black. And they've got piercings and tattoos and hair the color of snot. It's something. And we saw a show at the Mirage, or maybe Bally's. Really nice."

"Well, good," I say. "When did you get back?"

"We've been back a while," she says. She's probably been back a week but she doesn't want me to know that. "How are they?"

"About the same — still standing at the counter waiting on Bob to die so they can get some cheap chairs."

"What?" So I explain it to her. "Those two," she says in a disappointed tone. "Did they say anything about their will, getting it fixed?"

"Yeah, I'm going to take them in about two weeks."

"Two weeks." She says, disappointed. "I thought they were going to do it like the next day, the way they talked. Seems like a long time."

Whenever she thinks like I think, there's cause for alarm. One of us is in trouble.

"Does it matter?" I ask her.

"Oh, no, doesn't matter to me. Whenever," and there's a suspicious silence on her end. "So everything's okay? Need me to do something?"

"Somebody's got to take them shopping, probably tomorrow."

"Oh, I'm sorry. I can't tomorrow. I've got an interview at, about, eleven. Over at Tracer's. I really don't want to go back so soon, but I guess I'll give it a shot. Darnell says I should just forget about it for a month or so, but I feel bad so I'm going to see what they say."

She's lying. I know it. She doesn't even know the time of the interview. There's desperation for you.

"Well, good luck," and I play along. "Have you decided when you're going to tell them about you and Darnell?"

"I'm not even sure I'm going to tell them, and that's the truth." I believe her. Life's not complicated enough. We all need some useless lies to help out.

"You know, Brenda, it kind of puts me in a bad spot. I don't like knowing about it and not telling them, it's kind of dishonest. I don't understand why you don't just tell them. I mean, what can they do?"

"I'd just rather not. Darnell's already dealing with his mother and everything. I just don't want a big argument with them now. I'll tell them, just give me a while. Okay?"

This sucks. "All right, I'll give you a while, but a while is pretty soon. I'm not going to keep pretending that I don't know about it, and really, for no good reason. It's none of their business anyway. That's what you always say, so hell, tell them and they can just deal with it. Okay?"

"Okay, okay. I'll tell them, but don't say anything until I tell you. I'll do it pretty soon. Listen, give me a call if you need anything. I want to do my share and all. We love you guys. See you later."

"Goodbye," and I start to say Brenda, but she's gone.

#

They don't want to go shopping the next day, so we agree on the day after tomorrow. I ought to call Brenda and say, if you want to do your part take them shopping Thursday. No doubt she'll have an interview then too. I'd rather spare myself another lie and just do it.

I'm about to leave the house Thursday morning when they call. "Good news," says Dad.

"Oh yeah," I say. "What's up?"

"He died — day before yesterday. I'm going to get those stools, today maybe. So make sure you come on over. I want you to see them," and he's as excited as a kid with a new toy. I suppose he wouldn't be surprised if I let out a war-whoop to celebrate Bob's demise. This is not my dad. My dad would never feel this way about someone dying. This is an imposter who's taken his place beside the truly evil one. It has to be. I can't stand it any longer.

"Dad," I say, calmly, "I want you to listen to yourself. You're calling it great news because one of your neighbors died. I mean think about that. All because of some cheap stools? I mean would you want someone to feel that way about you? Happy you died because they got your, I don't know, dining room table? I mean come on. Are you going to send them some flowers or a card? I can't believe you feel that way."

"Well, now, that dining room table is worth a lot more than those chairs. You know that don'tcha?"

"That's not the point. Don't you see that?"

"Well, uh, what is the point?" he says. "I don't, uh, have anything to do with whether or not he, uh, lives. Everybody's got to go sometime and all their stuff will belong to, uh, somebody, won't it?"

I don't know why I even try. They're complete aliens. I must find a way to reconcile myself to this new couple from another universe. "Okay. I'm on my way."

When I get there, I'm shocked once again. Bob's son, my parent's missing child, has delivered the monstrosities to their garage. It's bright outside and looking into the garage is like looking into a tunnel – dark and foreboding. Despite the unfavorable optical conditions, I can see four glowing orange things lying on the garage floor. When I enter the garage, I realize that they are, indeed, cushions for the stools. Even worn and faded, they could attract attention from the furthest galaxy.

I go into the house from the garage and come down the hallway. Then I see the jumbled pieces of wrought iron assembled by a crack-head on a bad night. This is what they've purchased with their souls? They've given up their humanity for twisted rusty bent disagreeable cheap iron. There's no pattern or discernable theme to the giant ugly pieces that fit too tightly in the space allowed. The flat iron arms are only missing a leather belt to secure the condemned. Small tabs near the bottom of the front legs must be terminals for the electrical wires that I'm sure came with the original stools. I'm forced to wonder if the State Penitentiary at Greedsville has been robbed. They are hideous beyond description and worth at least two souls. It's funny how God works.

I shouldn't take any pleasure from this, and to my credit, I'm not. It's hard to take my view away from the static train wreck that has also forced them to move the dining room table over another foot. The once pretty picture of a small bridge that crosses a deep blue stream is now ugly, just by proximity. Then I realize that it's not centered over anything now. It's as though someone placed glue on the back and stuck it on the wall wherever it would look worst.

"Sissy! Is that you?" It's Mom's voice from the sunroom.

"Yes," I manage.

"Come here. It's your father. Back here."

I don't hurry. At first I back away, keeping an eye on the devilment masquerading as furniture. Then I turn and slowly head towards them. I know this is the picture room, but I avoid the bookshelves.

Dad's lying on the couch. His eyes are rolled back and his nose is sporting enough nasal hair to cover his entire head. He's pale white, and it takes a few seconds before he takes a shallow, shuttering breath.

"Call Beeler's," I tell Mom. She's holding the small white emergency call button in her right hand. She has a hard mean look on her face. She's frowning at him, angry that he's caused this trouble. "Mom," I say loudly, "call Beeler's!" She doesn't move.

I attempt to reach for the device, but she pulls away quickly. "He's all right," she says, "just tired. Are you okay Stanley?" she says in a menacing voice. He nods slightly.

"Think so," he barely manages.

"Push the damn button Mom," I tell her again.

"Just wait," she says. Once again I try to reach for it but she moves it away from me. "Now just you wait. He's tired from moving those chairs. Give him a minute. He'll recover. You'll see." But I'm not waiting.

I grab her wrist and twist it up. I pry the alarm button from her hand and hold down on the red button. Then I release it and push it several times. I hear a woman's voice.

"This is the front desk. We're sending help. If you can answer me, push the green button on the panel in the hallway. We're sending help. Can you speak to me?"

I move quickly to the panel. "Yes this is Mr. Ray's daughter. My dad is having a stroke or a heart attack I think. He's barely breathing. Hurry!"

"We're calling EMS and our people are on the way. They'll be there in a minute. Is your father breathing?"

"Very shallow. Just barely," I say, and I'm surprised by my own deliberateness and lack of agitation.

"Is he lying down?" I answer several more questions about open breathing, blockages, falls, etc.

When we're finished, I open the front door wide and rush back to Dad. Mom's standing there, frowning down at him. I pull the old coffee table away and start moving the recliner back. Two men come through the door. They're carrying a bunch of equipment – a tank of oxygen and a mask, a heart defibrillator, a box of tools, a blood pressure cuff. Mom backs away as they kneel down beside him. One man is listening to his chest while the other one probes his mouth and then positions the mask and turns on the oxygen. Dad's chest rises and the man adjusts something. It starts to move up more rhythmically.

I hear something and look back. Two women are coming in with a stretcher. All four of these angels are swarming over him and talking loudly back and forth in a medical emergency jargon that is incomprehensible to me. But I know what stabilize means, I just don't know if he is, or if that's what they're trying to do.

One of them is talking into a radio and reading from an electric chart that another one is holding up for her to see. I think she's talking with the EMS people.

As soon as she finishes, she looks at me. "Take her, and wait in there. Stay back. EMS is close. We're going to load him up," and she goes back to work. I grab Mom by the arm and pull her into her bedroom.

"Put on something decent," I order her. "We'll follow them out. Hurry." She's still got a disgruntled look on her face, but she turns toward the closet. I walk back out, but stop as they glide past me with Dad on the stretcher. One of them is still talking on the radio, and the rest are working in a harmony that would be the envy of the Tabernacle Choir.

I notice that tears are streaming down my face. Then Mom appears. She turns slowly as they pass through the front door. I think I can hear a siren. It has to be a world record for response time. The siren is getting louder and the volume is almost unbearable when it abruptly stops. I can see the flashing light against the door.

I grab her arm and lead her to the front. We watch him being transferred to another stretcher and then it's pushed into the back of the truck. A man turns and looks at me. "He can have one rider,' he shouts.

"No. Where are you taking him? We'll follow."

"We're going to East. Don't speed ma'am," and he slams the door and bolts for the front. I watch them turn around and then the siren goes back on, and they disappear around the corner.

Chapter 23: CCU Revelations

When we think of hospitals, we think of clean surfaces, scrubbed arms and hands, giant thick glass partitions, white smocks, crisp sheets, cold solid floors, stainless steel machinery, blinking lights, and silence. The CCU unit at East has all those things, but it also has antiseptic light. It's a blue-white light that permeates the entire area leaving no room for shadows.

Dad's peacefully reposed in his flexible bed with IV lines, heart monitors and oxygen inhalers strewn about his face and arms. Blinking boxes hover above him and occasional alarms disturb the reigning silence.

They say he's stable, but critical. He's too sick to undergo an operation on his enlarged heart. They call his stroke moderate, and I haven't noticed that he can't move his face like he used to. He's smiled a couple of times, but mostly he's slept.

He has this room to himself, and there's one recliner and one wooden chair. I've decided that he's got the best room in the ward – next to the back entrance, down the hallway from the main nurse's station. The glass windows that form the front wall have those tiny wires that form perfect diamonds that are really squares balancing on a bottom corner. The window is covered with mini-blinds that are unevenly spaced and poorly aligned. Mom has worked on them to no avail.

I've initialed the Living Will document they have on file. They'll take measures to keep him alive, but not extraordinary measures that will do his living for him. This is what he wanted.

I've made a half-dozen calls to Brenda, but I've concluded that she's comatose in her bed somewhere. I finally gave up and called Carolyn to see if she could reach Darnell. Each time the door opens I expect to see Bubbles swaggering through in a hurry to demonstrate her magnanimous care and love for her poor ill father. I'm confident that she'll put on an Oscar performance.

T2 and Brian have been in for a few minutes. They consoled Mom, and then T2 procured a wheelchair. They took her down to the cafeteria for a cup of coffee and a bagel. That was about five minutes ago.

An extremely large nurse comes to the door.

"Excuse me," she says, "we don't have an admitting physician. Do you know who his doctor is?"

"Can we use Dr. Ariswamy, that's his cardiologist?"

"Sure. Dr. Ari is fine. I'll let him know Mr. Ray is here. I'm sure he'll come by," and she plods off.

Theo comes back in with a diet drink.

"See anybody?" he asks as he sits down in the wooden chair.

"Just a nurse. I used Ariswamy as the admitting doctor. They don't have a family doctor now, or at least I don't know who it is."

"So, she wasn't going to call for help?" he says.

I shake my head in resignation. I want to believe that she was really undecided about whether or not it was serious. It's easy to look back and find our mistakes. Now we know it was, and she's mad at me for, I don't know what, wrestling the panic button from her I guess.

"He says she made him move the table. That's the first thing he said – 'She made me move the table – there'll be a third hole, you know that don'tcha?' and he went back to sleep. There's not much else they can do. Look at his oxygen," and I point at the digital readout. "Keeps falling below eighty. That's not good. And that's with the oxygen on."

We are silent for a minute. I sit on the edge of the recliner and we hold hands. I'm very composed and have been the whole time. "Everybody's got to go sometime," I say to myself. That's what Dad said—just this morning. I'm remembering what I said about not wanting to go to heaven if they were there. I'm remembering the two lost souls – lost to cheap chairs.

I'm not going to regret those thoughts. Mom and Dad brought them on by their own actions. But I am happy that I don't have a say in that decision. That's above my pay grade. That's His call. He's got the big job, and it's His decision. He knows better than to listen to me.

"Don't let her," says Dad in a low whisper that makes me stand up and lean over him.

"You'll be okay," I tell him. Theo stands up beside me.

"No," says dad. "Don't take her," and he's turned his head to look at me. "Okay?" he adds.

"You need to rest so you'll get better," I say quietly. His hand moves and I reach over and gently, carefully, squeeze his fingers. He tries to grip.

"Don't let her change it," and his stomach is rising from the effort to speak. I can detect a slight slur that goes beyond his tiredness. It's barely perceptible. "The will," he says. "Don't take her," and he closes his eyes. The blood oxygen count is flashing eighty-two. He doesn't need to talk yet.

"Okay," I say, and he squeezes my hand. Theo is giving me a perplexed look. I shrug my shoulders. Both of us heard what he said – don't let her change the will, don't take her. Those are his directions. This isn't what I want to think about now, but I have to wonder why it's important to him.

It sounds like he's gone back to sleep and the count goes up to eighty-four, so that's an improvement.

Theo and I sit back down. "That doesn't sound good," says Theo. "Sounds like she wants to change her will, but he doesn't want to. Of course, if he can't make it to the office, she can sign for him. Didn't you tell me that they each had power of attorney for the other one?"

"Yeah —full power — not just medical. The whole thing."

"You better find out what that's about. Hell, maybe she's cutting you out, giving it all to Brenda."

"I don't believe that," but I admit that I'm worried for the first time about their money. I want to think that I don't care about it, but it's not just the money, it's what they'd be saying by taking me out of the will. It's a real slap in the face.

Theo leaves when Mom gets back. He's got a dozen errands to run to get everything that we need. She's determined to change purses because this one doesn't have a closing zipper, just a snap type buckle.

Mom settles into the recliner. She'll hardly look at me, and I suppose it's about this morning.

"I hope she's okay," she suddenly says.

"What?"

"I hope Brenda's okay. Something must be wrong."

"We've had trouble reaching her before. I'm sure she's fine. I've called every number I have. I told you I called Darnell's sister. That's all I know to do."

"She ought to be here," she says, and she's right. Brenda shouldn't just drop off the edge of the earth whenever she wants to. Responsible people don't do that, but she's not responsible.

I can hear some activity out in the area by the vacant auxiliary nurse's station that they use for patients on this end of CCU.

As I stand up to go out, a woman comes to the door.

"Hello," she says, "I'm Doctor Weller. I'm with Dr. Ariswamy. Dr. Ari is backed up in the Cath Lab."

We shake hands.

"Hi. I'm Sissy Woodson. That's my dad," and I nod toward the bed. "And this is my mom," as Mom tries to fight her way out of the recliner.

"You don't need to get up," says Dr. Weller as she steps over to Mom. She extends her hand and Mom relaxes back into the chair, but makes no effort to shake.

"How's he doing?" I ask, but I can already tell from the look on Dr. Weller's face that it's not good.

"Your father is not well. He has an enlarged heart, what we call cardiomegaly, and it's really struggling now. It's a symptom of his hypertension, and of course his previous heart attack. We've done an Echocardiogram and Ultrasound. It was already weak, and it was injured this morning which is what led to his stroke. If he were younger and in better overall health, we could consider an operation, but as your father has been told before, that's not possible here," and she's looking at me, and then glancing at Mom. "I wish there were more we could do. We're going to try to get some fluid off of him and see if that doesn't help him. Do you have any questions?"

"When can he leave?" asks Mom, harshly.

Dr. Weller glances at me quickly before she says, "That's hard to estimate right now. We'll have to see how he comes along."

I already know that he may not come out of here at all, and if he does it'll be to a nursing home. I don't think he's going back home. I look from Dad to her. "Will he be staying in CCU?"

"I think so. They could move him if beds become a problem, but it doesn't look like that. Dr. Ari will probably be through later, if not I'll check back in with you."

A nurse comes in and hands her a clipboard. Dr. Weller looks it over and says, "Thanks," as she hands it back. The nurse says, "We were ready to change it over," and Weller says, "That's fine. Go ahead." The nurse nods and walks out of the room.

"Well," she says, and she looks at Mom, "I'm sorry about your husband. When you see the amount of damage he suffered in his heart attack, what, twenty-five years ago, he's really had to work to keep himself in such good shape. If there's anything we can do for you, just let the nurse know," and she shakes my hand again as she leaves.

She's hardly got away when Mom says, "Wash your hands, Sissy."

"Why?"

"Sissy!" she says, and she drags my name out in total exasperation, "you know why."

"No I don't," and I'm looking at her.

"You shook her hand twice."

"She's dirty?" I ask.

"She's a damn negro Sissy. They all are, around here. I'm not coming to this place. Nurse was too."

I don't know why I continue to be astonished by her. And I don't know why I make any attempt to teach. It must be frustration or something.

"You're a racist, Mom. That's all that is – racism. Did you belong to the Klan? I never knew that."

"I ain't touched one in my life and I ain't starting now. Do what I said and wash your hands."

But I don't. Instead, I walk over to her recliner, I spread my arms out with both palms open to her face, and I slowly bring them together. She's squishing back in the recliner trying to get away, but I just keep moving them toward her until I'm within an inch of either cheek and she's got nowhere to go. I hold my position and look at her frightened face. I ought to shove my hand down her old throat, but I back up.

"You're a sick woman. Very sick. I'm going to get a drink," and I start out.

"It's too bad for you," she says. I hesitate, but decide to ignore her and head through the door. "I promise that," she shouts at me.

Chapter 24: Room 6L-66

I can only guess that Brian notified St. Vincent's and somebody there notified Father Vincenzo. He's the priest assigned to administer to the sick at Baptist-Haywood East. He meets me in the busy waiting room outside of CCU. He's very short and thick, but has a bright smile that anyone would envy.

We have a nice talk, and he and Theo exchange some Latin. Theo must tell him a broken Latin joke of some kind because he smiles and points his finger at Theo as if to admonish him playfully. I walk down the hall with him and explain as gently as I can why it might be better if he didn't visit Dad's room. I think he's used to this, and he motions for Theo and leads us in a prayer right there in the hall.

Mom's in a better mood than she was. I'm not sure if anything happened while I was boycotting her presence, but when I return she is anxious to talk about their funeral plans. It's the healthiest exchange I've had with her in quite some time. Then I discover that a Baptist minister has come through and spent some time with her and Dad. I'm not sure what he told her, but it's had a pleasant effect.

"We'll just do it at Mallory's. He says they have a beautiful service chapel," she tells me. I might discourage her from such pessimistic talk, but Dad's numbers are falling and the nurses have reset the alarm a couple of times. I'm no Brenda fan, but I'm praying she gets here before he dies. I make a point not to mention her, but it's nearly ten pm. Visiting hours ended at nine.

The waiting room is nearly empty except for a couple of families who must have no place to go, or who's loved one is very close to death. One family sits in the near corner, silent and resigned. The other one has taken over the area next to the vending machines. I hate to judge people by their attire and mannerisms, but it's hard not to.

The two men look to be nearly sixty. One of them is wearing work cloths, and I can see a name tag sewn onto his shirt. He looks thin, except he has that distended belly that, on a woman, would signify pregnancy. The other guy is thin and bald. He's wearing scruffy jeans and an old t-shirt that has some band's tour dates listed on the back. A faded guitar on the front has 'Believe.' scribbled on it.

The two women are Brenda-esque in size. Their clothes were obviously purchased when they were much smaller and nary a roll goes unseen. Some younger kids with long straggly hair and giant baggy pants keep coming and going as does the whole group, two at a time. I hear them say that they're going out for a smoke, but when they come back they've always got something to eat.

I can't help imagining that Darnell looks like the guy with the guitar t-shirt. Only his shirt will have a truck on the front and the mud-flap girl on the back. And he'll have that giant belt-buckle that resembles a hubcap on a fifty-nine Ford, like the guy I watched walk into the Oasis Club that day.

Theo has returned with all the junk we sent him out for. Mom's pacified now that she has her impregnable zippered purse. I've tried to reach Brenda on Theo's cell, thinking she won't recognize that number, but we still haven't heard from her. Carolyn called to say that she couldn't reach Darnell, but that she'd keep trying. She's very consoling on the phone.

Mom's planning to spend the night. She has her bag of stuff that she said she needed. I'm hanging on, waiting for Brenda. The CCU has strict rules on visitors – no more than two at a time and only during visitation hours. But they never stop me from coming and going, and Theo, Mom and I have all been in Dad's room at the same time.

I've told Mom that Theo and I are going to be out in the waiting room, and that we hope to reach Brenda. She just grunts and mumbles something under her breath. Brenda has no idea the pain she's causing now.

Theo is wearing a headlamp. I'm serious. It's one of those hat-band lights that shine wherever you look. He has a box full of papers that he's buried himself in. He's one of those people who can work anywhere, and the CCU waiting room is fine with him. But we both jump when his cell rings.

When he starts to fish it out of the holder on his belt, that stupid light goes everywhere. "Turn that off." I whisper angrily. He pulls it off his head and lays it in the box, still shining across to the doors into the unit, while trying to get to his phone.

"Hello," he says, and then he pauses. "Yeah, you'll probably have to come through the front now, but you can go out those doors. They're right in front of you, third floor. There's a big arrow that says CCU. Okay," and he ends the call.

"That's Brenda. She's on her way up."

I roll my eyes and lean back into the chair. "Finally. Thank God she made it. I was beginning to really worry."

We wait another five minutes. I'm just about to go out to find her when she turns out of the elevator hall into the long hallway. She's wearing a pants suit instead of her sweats. I meet her as she nears us and we hug. I can smell pot all over her so I know that's what took a while.

"Sorry. We set our damned phones down in the cup holders and forgot all about them. How's he doing?" and she sees Theo. "Hi honey," she says and gives him a hug.

I tell her about Dad as we walk down the long hall that goes behind the ward to the back entrance, nearest his room. You have to buzz yourself in from the front, but you can just walk in from back here. I'm hoping they didn't lock the door, but it opens into the CCU and we're bathed in that antiseptic light.

I'm surprised to find Mom sound asleep in the recliner. She says she never sleeps because of her pain, but it must have subsided inside this germ-free environment. Her head is tilted, mouth open, and if I didn't know better I would check her pulse.

"Mom, Mom," I say quietly. Then I shake her arm and her eyes flash open. Her head turns slightly until she sees us.

"Oh. Thank God," she says, struggling to get out of the chair. Brenda is hovering over Dad. She comes around and gives Mom a kiss and they hug ferociously like a returning military man and his pregnant wife. Brenda is crying, and tears are streaming down her face. Mom's saying "there, there," and she produces one of her magic trick tissues. Brenda wipes her face, and together they stand over his bed.

The small red 'Low O2' light is blinking silently. It's at seventy-eight. I stand across from them, and all three of us are looking down at Dad. He seems so calm and comfortable. His chest barely rises every few seconds.

Brenda is leaning against the bed rail, and I can see it bending in. I hope they didn't get it from the lowest bidder.

"Darnell couldn't come," says Brenda. "He had to work tonight. He sends his best though," and Mom nods like she knows Darnell well. My first thought is that he works second shift, and I wonder how that comports with the cup-holder cell phones? I don't want to hear it.

"Listen," I tell them. "We've been here all day. We're going to head out. You have my number. If there's a change, or you need something, call me."

I walk around and give them both a kiss. "If I don't hear from you, I'll be back in the morning."

As I'm heading down the hall I'm thinking how appropriate it is that Brenda should be stuck here with Mom. I should be thinking about Dad, but I can't help wonder how long Brenda will hang on here. I decide that that's between her and Mom. They can work it out. Theo and I get home around eleven.

#

It's only six-forty-five, but I'm on my second cup of coffee when the phone rings. It's a teary, groggy Brenda. They're moving Dad to a regular room and they've told them that they should think about calling in the family. So this is it.

I don't rush. I'm reconciled to it. Theo decides to drive over by himself. I think my comments about 'Bob' hanging on for an extra week or so have given him the idea that he needs to maintain an independent mobile capability. Plus, he knows that any errands will fall to him, and he'd rather have his own car.

He follows me into the parking lot, and we go up to the sixth floor, room 6L-66. It's bright and sunny up here. Mom's asleep in another recliner. I think I'll recommend that she uses that at home.

We sneak around to his bedside and just stand there looking down at him. He's still hooked up to all the same equipment as best I can tell, but it's spread out, and this room is at least twice the size of the one in CCU. There's a huge bank of windows, and we're lucky to be on the west side. I can see the shadow of this building on the east wall of the parking garage.

There's no Brenda, and I'm wondering if she's gone home, wherever that is. We stand there for a few minutes whispering back and forth. I can tell that if we don't make some noise, she could sleep all day. Then Brenda comes sauntering through the big wooden door. She's got a bag from the cafeteria.

"Morning," she says. Now I see why she wears sweats. Her lavender outfit has more creases than an accordion. Her hair's a mess – a mutilated mullet. She sets the bag down on the rolling table. "I've been here all night," she announces. I suppose she wants some sympathy, but she won't get it from me.

I look back down at Dad. "I know. We were here more than twelve hours yesterday. It wears you out, waiting around. I guess it doesn't look too good, but his numbers look the same."

"I don't know," she says. "I don't think he's going to come out of this. I wish you could have reached me yesterday so I could have talked to him, you know, one last time, maybe."

Perhaps I'm a little sensitive, but it sounds like we didn't try hard enough to contact her. I let it pass. Mom comes to, and she struggles to get out of her seat.

"Can I help you?" says Theo, extending a hand. But she ignores him and fights to get herself up. She creaks over to his bed.

"That Ariswamy came by," she says. "He doesn't know a thing. Just said they did all they could. So I guess he's given up. Probably what they do over there, where he's from," and she looks down at Dad. "I told him to find someone else, but he wouldn't listen. He liked the Indian. So see where it got you?" she says to Dad.

I look at Brenda and shake my head in resignation. She's an equal opportunity bigot. I wonder immediately how long Dad was lying on that sunroom couch before I wrestled the alarm from her – one minute, twenty minutes? Who knows, and you'd never get the truth out of her. Theo is right, when she meets her maker she better hope he's the New Testament God, not the Old Testament God.

"I got some bagels and coffee," says Brenda. "I'm starving. Place doesn't open up until six. You'd think in a hospital it would be open twenty-four, seven. You can't live off those damn vending machines down there."

I recall a story I heard years ago about two guys who decided to try an experiment with marijuana. They wanted to find out what would happen if you smoked a joint every day for a month. What they discovered was that two guys can eat all the Doritos in Phoenix in one month.

As I look at Brenda, I wonder; between the pot and the cigarette breaks and the vending machine runs, when did she find time to sleep?

Mom looks at Theo. "Can you find me a wheelchair like, like they did?" she asks. "Maybe I could get outside for a few minutes and then get some toast. Brenda and Sissy can take me if you're going to be around a while."

"Sure," says Theo, and he leaves.

"You don't want a bagel?" says Brenda.

"Get it downstairs," says Mom. "Theo can have them."

It takes a few minutes before Theo returns with the granddaddy of all wheelchairs. It's high-backed, mostly wooden, and has padded arms and seat. He helps her sit down.

"Let's go," she orders.

Brenda takes us to an outside area designed for smokers. It sets in the middle of several buildings, but well away from any entrances. There's absolutely no shade to be had, and we're lucky it's still early or this place would be an oven.

"I'm going to need some help," says Mom to both of us. "Somebody needs to go to Mallory's and pick out the stuff. Get everything ready in case your father doesn't make it," and she's very business-like. "Get a Baptist to do the service. Make sure. Don't let them talk you into nothing. Don't spend too much on a casket, Stanley wouldn't like that, but get a good vault. A good one. And not too much on flowers either. People will send them."

Yeah, sure, all your friends. But it's obvious that she's given this some thought. I don't care who does it, but I'll be shocked if it's Brenda. I'm not going to say a word. She continues with a list of things like memorial books and prayer cards and which suit to buy and music during the service. They all have one thing in common – don't. Don't pay extra for anything that involves dressing him up and boxing him up — except she wants a nice vault. I thought they were all big concrete boxes that covered the casket, but apparently you can get a better, what, concrete mix?

"Well, Mom," says Brenda. "I've been here all night. I'm worn out. I'm going to have to ask Sissy to do this," and she looks at me. I shrug and look at Mom.

"Okay, Sissy can do it." It's not a request, it's an order. I have been assigned.

"Don't you want to look at anything?" I ask her. "I mean maybe Brenda can get some rest and come back and stay here, and I can take you over there, and we can look at everything together. Probably won't take an hour or two at the most."

She shakes her head. "Nope. You're his favorite. You'll do it fine. Just remember he wouldn't spend too much."

"Oh mother!" I say, and I look at Brenda and shake my head. "How much are you talking about? Do you have any idea? And what about the limos to Harmon? Do you want to make those arrangements too? All this stuff is pretty expensive, so I need some idea about how much you're thinking," and that 'favorite' comment just begs for a slam, but I don't.

"Just whatever Stanley would spend. You know him," she says. She's so ridiculous. And I'm not about to do anything until we agree on some idea of what she thinks.

"No," I say forcefully. "I don't know what he would spend on his own funeral, and I'm not doing a thing until we agree on some idea about what this will cost. Now do you have any idea?"

"Can't you decide?" she says.

"We're going to decide right now," I tell her. "It's expensive as hell to bury someone today – ten, fifteen thousand dollars. Something like that," and I hear her gasp. "So is that what you're thinking?"

"That's for a gold casket," she says.

"No it isn't. That's why you're going with me. You can sit there and let them go over all the prices with you. But you're crazy if you think I'm going to go and pick everything out, then have you refusing to pay because it's too much. So we'll just go together. That way you'll know."

She's so mad she's shaking even more than usual. She looks at Brenda. "Can you do it?"

"I am just beat. My feet are killing me," says Brenda. "Sorry," then she looks at me. "Ten thousand dollars?" she asks.

"Probably more than that," I tell her. "Of course we can bury him in a pine box if you want to save money. And we can rent a U-Haul to get him to Harmon. And, Brenda, you and Darnell can dig the damned hole. So it can be done cheaper."

We stand here silently. Mom's stewing and Brenda just wants to get out of here. But there's no damn way I'm going to end up paying for it. No way.

Her head's moving around, making that pecking motion. She's thinking about how she's going to get her way.

"Look, Mom, this is simple. It won't take us long, and you can get exactly what you want."

"No," she says. "Between ten and fifteen. No more than fifteen, okay? It's robbery. Damn people."

I look at Brenda. "Did you hear that? She said no more than fifteen thousand dollars. Did you hear her?" Brenda barely nods, but says nothing. I look at Mom. "Okay. If that's what you insist. But I don't want to hear a bunch of griping at the funeral, assuming there is one. I won't try to spend that much, but I know it costs a lot. Okay?"

"I'm ready to go back. I hope Theo left me a bagel."

"I'm not going back up," says Brenda. "I'm about to drop. I'll check in tonight." She bends over and gives Mom a kiss. She gives me a harsh look. "See you later."

I nod and grab this damned big-ass wheelchair and head back to his room.

Chapter 25: Hallway Epiphany

I could write another whole book about the saintly mobsters that run the funeral business. Bereavement Business, I should say. Theo and I make all the choices, and Mom didn't know the half of them. Nevertheless, since we didn't have to buy plots, we do it okay for eight dollars under ten thousand.

No Brenda last night. She called about seven to check on him. That was so considerate of her.

I took Mom over to our house yesterday late afternoon, after Theo and I got back from Mallory's. Theo stayed with Dad who doesn't move at all except for his small breaths.

She got a bath and rested on the sofa in the living room. She was actually complimentary about my decorating. It must have killed her. But she wants to go back to the hospital, and I can understand that. I've offered to take her back to Beeler's, but she refuses.

I talked to Mom this morning and his condition is unchanged, except his oxygen is down.

"Brenda is coming," she tells me. I decide to go on in. Since Darnell works afternoons, it would seem logical for Brenda to come out later and stay till ten or so. Now it sounds like she wants day-watch. Fine, I'm flexible. I'll run in for a while and then come back later.

Ali called, and she's sorry she couldn't make it with T2. She wonders if this morning is a good time. We agree to meet for breakfast at Simms Café. She has proofs of a new Find-a-Cure pamphlet she'd like for me to see before it goes to press.

We have wonderful Eggs Benedict and strong black chicory flavored coffee — way too much for either one of us — but delicious just the same. We park beside each other and go up to the room.

Mom's sitting in a chair looking out the bank of windows. "They've already been through," she says. "Where's Brenda?" she asks.

"I don't know. You said she was coming."

She mumbles.

It's all I can do to get her to tell me what the doctor said. She's more interested in demeaning his continent. Ali is very gracious and stays about twenty minutes. I walk her back down to her new Mercedes SUV which looks a whole lot like an impractical minivan to me, but I know it's expensive.

Theo calls and I give him an update. While I'm talking to him, I spot a wheelchair of less staggering proportions than the one we had yesterday. I stop at the nurse's station and ask for an update on Dad and permission to use the wheelchair. They gave him a bath last night and tried to get him to sit up, but he's on some pain medication and he's comfortable. They angled his bed for several hours to help him drain better.

I park the wheelchair in the hallway, right by the door. I can hear Brenda inside.

". . . says it's ready. They'll print it today. You can go down and sign it tomorrow."

I feel a little bad about eavesdropping, but I can't get the brake set on this wheelchair, so I'm fooling with it while paying close attention to their conversation. "Have you told Sissy about this?" asks Brenda.

"I told you to," says Mom, then she adds, "none of her business anyway. It's my money now. It's all legal." She's mumbling something else, but I can't hear her.

I can feel the change in my physiology. They're talking about the will. "Don't take her," Dad said. "Don't let her change it, the will," he whispered. I have the fleeting thought that Theo won't make a good witness.

Now I'm trying to decide if I want to bring this up. I know I'm going to, I just don't know where. It seems disrespectful to argue about it right in front of Dad even though he probably doesn't hear or know anything. I can feel a little of the lightheadedness that attended my blackout. I sit down in the wheelchair and take a few deep breaths. I know it looks stupid to be sitting here in the hallway, but I just need to gather myself. I doubt that Brenda has engineered this, but she's going along with it. I remember Mom saying, "It's too bad for you. I promise that." I have to think this was what she was talking about. But I can't figure out what kind of change she's making. I know it was in the works before our last run-in because the appointment was already set for next week. Now Brenda's saying it will be ready tomorrow. Maybe I'm conjuring up this conspiracy, but Dad's warning is still lying there in my head like a bowling ball in a wallet. I know what Theo thought. He's not screwed up.

I'm worried about developing tunnel vision, but I don't see it yet. I can see a sign down the hall that says 'Exit' and somehow that word sounds so good to me. I close my eyes and there's a kind of flickering before things start to clear up. It's bright behind my eyeballs – too bright. Then I see a cool shady spot in each eye. When I concentrate, it comes into focus and my two palm trees are gently swaying back and forth.

I've decided that this is the actual physical picture of mental illness for Sissy Woodson. I'm sure it's different for someone else, but this is it for me. I'm afraid to open my eyes – I'll lose my palm trees, and probably start the tunnel view of earth. I know I'm sitting in a wheelchair on the sixth floor of East outside room 6L-66, Dad's room. I know I'm upset about this will business. I know I'm facing a confrontation with Mom and probably with Bubbles as well. I know I'm suffering from anxiety. I try to remember what Selvey said. I concentrate on her professional face. I can see the covers of several books on the subject. I chuckle when I think about those covers. If I make it through this, I'm going to email the publishers and warn them that they must remove those grainy drawn frenzied pictures of lines and colors that are the artistic symbols of anxiety. It is imperative that they replace them with pictures of beautiful scenery, like sunrise over the Serengeti, or a cool mountain stream amidst giant redwoods. Out of focus zig-zaggy lines are no help. Dumbasses. Obviously they haven't suffered from the disease.

I know now that I've tried to avoid any thought at all about their money, like it was somehow, I don't know, *tacky* is the word Mom would use. I also know that I'm the one who has been trying to get them to spend the damn money. What's the point of it if you don't use it?

But then I think about Mom. I've got it all wrong. Theo and I always joked about, 'can't take it with you.' But that's the wrong approach with her. She doesn't want to take it with her; she's not that stupid. And she doesn't want to spend it. Now I know why. She intends to use it as a weapon. To her it's like having an extra two million warheads. You never know when they'll come in handy. That's why she holds on to it so ferociously. It's just a weapon. So this is good. I figured it out sitting here in this wheelchair with my palm trees. Now that I know, I must formulate a counter-offensive.

I know this; her weapon only works against me and Brenda. It's impotent outside of that theater of engagement. She's already used it on Bubbles, and it's a potent weapon for a dumb fat girl who stays high all the time just to deal with her mom, and who hasn't got a future regardless of the money.

I'm not dumb, and I have a good future. So if I'm bright, I'll figure out a way to handle this. The exact strategic response will depend on the battlefield conditions, but I suddenly realize that I can win this war, since I understand my enemy's tactics and purpose. I resolve to engage my adversary. It's not even going to be a fair fight.

I promise myself.

Now I must open my eyes and mount my trusty steed. I'll ride between the swaying palms and defeat her on the beach.

I see the 'Exit' sign and the glassy reflection of shiny linoleum. I take a deep breath and push myself out of the wheelchair. I stand here, waiting to see if my internal systems are functioning properly. I hear someone behind me.

"Excuse me ma'am. Are you okay?" says a nurse, or somebody in a uniform. She's cute as can be with a bright smile. On her pocket is a broach. It's a colorful set of palm trees with 'kids' embossed below the trees making a beach. It's small, but beautiful.

"Oh," I say. "Yes. I'm fine. That's a beautiful pin."

She smiles. "It's for our 'Kid's March,'" she says. This Saturday. Raising funds for research."

"So you have sponsors?"

"Yeah, you know, a dollar a mile for five miles. Just whatever."

"That's nice. I've done that before," I tell her. I reach into my purse and pull out my billfold. I grab a ten. "Here. You take this. Make sure you finish, okay?"

"You can give it to me after the walk," she says.

"That's all right," I tell her. "I trust you," and I give her a shallow hug.

"Well, that's so nice," she says. "Thank you."

I nod and start to enter the room. "Wait, wait," she says and she reaches into her pocket. She pulls out one of the pins. "Here." She reaches up to my lapel. "Oh, that is pretty. I've never really looked at it, so thank you twice. It matches your outfit." We shake hands.

"I'll wear it like a shield," I tell her. She nods and walks away.

Inside the room, Brenda is chewing on a Three Musketeers bar. Mom is staring out the window. She turns to look at me. "That didn't take long," she says, like it didn't take long enough to suit her.

"I've got a wheelchair, if you want to go outside for a while?" I see Brenda nod.

"Yeah," says Brenda. "I need a cigarette."

"Okay," says Mom. She looks at Brenda. "They're bad for you," she says.

"I know," says Brenda. "Darnell and I are going to quit. Soon as everything settles down."

I roll it in and we go directly to the smoking place. I turn Mom to face into the sun. Brenda sits on a chair beside her and I face both of them.

No one is around. The place becomes suddenly shady as a big cloud passes over. It's a sign to begin.

"I heard you two talking about the will. Did they get it done early?" Brenda hiccups. Mom starts rubbing her hands together, but this time it doesn't look like worry. It looks more like, anticipation – as if she's getting ready to dig in to a nice dessert.

"It's fixed the way your Dad wanted it," says Mom. Brenda looks on anxiously.

"It's funny," I say. "Theo and I were talking with dad right after they brought him in. He kept saying, 'Don't let her change it. Don't take her.' That's what he said. 'The will, don't let her change it.' So did you change it?"

I lean back against a concrete bench. My shadow covers Mom.

"I don't know what he said," says Mom. "I just know what we agreed to and that's the final thing. What we agreed to."

"So, what did Dad and you agree to?" I'm not going to fool around here. "Do you have the guts to tell me?"

"It's up to me," she says, loudly. "We saved it. It's up to what I want to do. Your father is not able to sign it, so the lawyer says I can sign for him. Tomorrow. You don't have to take me, Brenda will. Right?" She looks around to Brenda.

"Whatever you think," says Brenda. "It's up to you." I can see her cigarette shake as she takes it up to her mouth. She needs better pot.

I just ignore her. She's well under the boot now.

"That's fine," I say. "I agree. It's your money and you can do with it whatever you please. So what do you please?" It's a challenge. I challenge you to use your weapon.

"You don't need it," she says. "Brenda's lost her job. It's going to her. That's final, like your dad agreed."

"So no fifty-fifty," I say, "just one hundred percent to Brenda. Is that it?"

"That's it," she says. Brenda tosses her cigarette to the ground.

"And you're okay with that?" I ask Brenda.

"Whatever she says, I guess. If that's what they want."

"And do you think that's fair?" I ask her. She tries to hide behind a new cigarette. The sun peaks out briefly and hits her in the face before disappearing again.

"It's what I want," says Mom.

I turn to her. "I didn't ask you. I'm asking Brenda," and I look back.

"Well, it wasn't fair the way they had it," says Brenda.

"And how did they have it?" I ask Mom.

"It was complicated," she says. "You were the Executrix, so it was kind of up to you. Now it's clear. We left you the bedroom suit and those pictures. That's plenty," and her cold dark calculating face is rigid, determined.

"Okay," I say. "So, how much are we talking about here?" I'm for getting down to the facts. I know it's a substantial sum of money from Dad's hints. "Do you know Brenda?"

"Mom would have to say," she deflects. Sweat traces a line down both sides of her face. She mops her forehead with her wrist.

"More than you think," says Mom. "A lot more."

Since I've figured out my adversary, I know she's going to tell me the exact amount. She probably knows it to the penny .

"Well?" I say and I look at her. "How much of this inheritance is there? If it's a hundred thousand dollars then, fine, she can have it. Is it more than that?"

That's an insult that she'll find hard not to answer. My battlefield maneuvering requires that she tells me exactly how much money she has. My response will be the same, regardless of the amount. But she has to do it. To hurt me, in her eyes, requires that I know exactly how much my independence is going to cost me. She's charging me for Theo. It's an independence tax. To get the full satisfaction, I need to be told the price.

"A lot more," she brags. "A lot more than that. But you don't need it," and she smiles a self-satisfying smirk. The cloud passes, and I move just enough that sunlight hits her in the face. She blinks, raises her hand and tilts her head away.

"Well, I might need it, if it's a lot. But I don't need a little. You're right. A hundred thousand or so means nothing to me, and Brenda needs it anyway. So fine."

She laughs, and if Disney had it on tape it would be worth all the money she has. It's an evil cackling laugh that reminds me that Satan is at work in all things.

"So you want to know how much?" she asks.

For strategic purposes only. I don't really need to know the extent of your hatred. I saw that when you fought to hold on to the alarm button.

"Absolutely," I say. "I mean, if you can't tell me how much you have, what would it be worth to you? Nothing, right?"

That made her mad. I can see it. She stiffens up.

"You'll see," she says, "if you live long enough."

She's like any good general; she doesn't want to roll out the big gun and expose it if she doesn't have to.

Brenda is occupied with her cigarette and the damp tissue she's managed to rescue from a pocket. She doesn't look up as she folds the tissue, then mops her cheeks and her upper lip, then folds it again.

I stand up. "Your money doesn't mean a thing to me. I don't care how much you have. I'll see you in the room." It's a bluff. I want this over with, and she wants to torture me – control me with the threat. I start to walk away.

"Sissy!" she says.

"What now?" I ask harshly, looking down at her. "What do you want?"

"Are you sure you want to know how much?" she says.

"Of course I'm sure." I give my shadow back to her. It's like a gift that I can bestow and withdraw.

"You might not want to know."

"I'm willing to risk it. Are you?"

She's smiling in her glory and power. The sudden satisfaction of telling me what I've lost is the same to her as a line of coke is to an addict. It's irresistible.

"What would you think if I told you it was nearly two million dollars?"

I look at Brenda. I think she knows this amount. At least she wasn't bought off cheap.

Once again, I subtract the shade. "I'd think you were lying because I know that you know exactly what it is, and when you tell me the truth it'll be to the penny. That's what I think. I'll see you around." I start off again.

"One million eight-hundred and eleven thousand dollars. I checked it. Course it's grown a little since then, since last week. So, now you happy?"

Finally, her big gun is fully exposed.

"Well, let me tell both of you something, and Brenda, this is for you, especially; Theo made more than that last year. He's pretty good with stocks and stuff. Always has been. Plus, T2 wants to buy a place in Florida. It'll cost him ten times that much, but he's got more money than God. As a matter of fact, one-point-eight million won't pay for the lot, much less the house. So like I said before, I don't care how much money you have. You can take it and stick it up Brenda's big fat ass for all I care." I start to walk away, then turn back as though I just remembered something.

"Oh. I almost forgot." I bend down and kiss Mom on her forehead. "Goodbye. I mean I'll see you at the funeral, but it's over with. After he's buried, I'll never see either one of you again. I have a life to live. A real life. Not a life smoking dope like fat ass here, or a life filled with hatred like you – a real life with a real family that has real love for each other. You can't buy that. Not even with their money, Brenda. And Mom, I'm sure Brenda will take care of you. She won't have to work if you'll string her along with some gifts, and she's always been so dependable. So you'll be fine.

"As a matter of fact, it's a great relief to me. I'm done fooling with both of you. It's like I'm completely free. Thank God for that. Praise Allah. Halleluiah." I start to leave again.

"Don't be like that," says Brenda.

I stop and turn on her. "Let me ask you something. Were you going to share that money with me?"

"Well, like you said, you don't need it." She's fidgeting around and staring at the dark purple sweat spots accumulating on her chest.

"I mean before you knew that?" I'm waiting, but she's already answered the question. "I didn't think so. You're an open book to an idiot. Both of you can rot in hell. Goodbye."

I take one last look at Mom. She's looking straight ahead with the blank stare of a zombie. I don't think this was as much fun as she thought it was going to be. I think she thought I'd cry and whine about the injustice of it all.

It's gone exactly as my epiphany directed – my hallway, wheelchair epiphany. I meant every word I said, even the lies. They'll never have the satisfaction of knowing where I exaggerated.

Chapter 26: Mallory's Surprise

I go back to the room and give Dad a kiss. I hold his hand and pray to God to forgive me for my comments about heaven. Dad's been a victim, just like me. More culpable perhaps, but still a victim.

I also thank God that Dad didn't have to see us. If his heart doesn't kill him, that probably would. So, all-in-all, this is a better way. I don't look at his numbers.

As I turn to leave, I see Mom's purse strap barely showing between the pillow and blankets stacked in the top of the built-in closet. I get it down, open it up and take out her checkbook. She shows a balance of eight-hundred and sixty-three dollars. That's not nearly enough, but that's her problem. I take out two checks. One is for Mallory's, and the other is for the limo company. I'll write the checks, and she'll have to refuse to sign them. I leave her a note saying that I took them, and that she'll need to transfer the funds to cover the funeral cost. I leave it sitting on the rolling table.

The full effect sets in back at the house. I just told Mom to take her money and shove it – literally. I even gave her directions. A deposit butt, so to speak. Now I have to tell Theo. He's always full of pompous principle-izing, so he'll just have to take it. There's a cost to your positions. But a million dollars is a lot of principle to shove around. I'm not really worried. My head's clear and I feel like the proverbial great weight has been lifted.

As soon as the funeral is over, I'm going to secretly plan a trip to the Bahamas – surprise Theo. Sheldon and Deidra are practically begging to go. I'll get with them. I need some palm trees. Then, if Brian goes to CERN, I'm going to plan a trip to Europe next year. I'm already looking forward to it. I'm free. Free of her.

The phone rings and I don't even look at the number.

It's Bubbles, crying and blathering. He's gone.

Okay, I tell her. "I'll get with Mallory's and make the arrangements." I look at my watch. "There's plenty of time to get the obituary into tomorrow's paper. We'll have visitation day after tomorrow from nine till two. That's how we planned it. The funeral will follow immediately, and we'll take him out to Harmon. So we'll do it all in one day. There's nobody from out of town to wait on. I'll see you and Mom at the funeral home."

"Are you," sniff, sniff, "going to come up," sniff, sniff, "here?"

"No. I saw him before I left. I'll see both of you, day after tomorrow at Mallory's. And Brenda, don't be late and don't have any excuses. Nine am until two, then the service. You got it?"

"Yes," sniff, "I got it."

"That'll give you all day tomorrow to get the will signed. I know how important that is. Goodbye."

"She," sniff, sniff, "wants to wait till after the funeral."

"That's totally up to you two. Do whatever you want. I'll see you."

"Sissy," sniff, sniff, "aren't you going to come and see her? It's your mom." sniff, sniff.

"If anything changes I'll let you know. This is exactly what we worked out with Mallory's. And no, I'll see her at Mallory's. Make sure she's there. That's the plan. I'll call if something changes. Goodbye Brenda," and I cut her off.

I will say this for Mom; she's taught me how to distance myself. It turns out that's handy.

#

"Ouch." That's what Theo keeps saying about my principled position: Ouch. Ouch. OUCH! He laughs when I tell him about how much he makes in the stock market. "So, I'm doing good?" he says. "That's our story?"

You got it Buster. Apparently it's worth a million dollars to me to deny her the satisfaction of controlling me with money. It's not fair to me or to Theo, I know that. But I'm actually looking forward to driving away from the cemetery in Harmon and knowing that I'm done with Mom and Brenda. And I am done.

Now I worry that Mom will change her mind about the will. I hope not. I don't want to have to turn it down a second time, but I will. I've gone the extra thousand miles for her, and for Brenda. I'm through. It feels good.

#

The obituary makes this morning's paper. The list of his memberships is short – exactly zero. The place and times are correct. It seems incredible that we should have to notify the entire city and half the state that somebody they don't care about has passed away. I think there are some legal reasons for doing this. If nothing else, it's on record.

Mallory's is non-denominational, part of some big conglomerate. I meet with them and give them the checks. They don't want me to fill in anything. They attach the checks to his folder and they use my credit card as security. Theo warned me about it, but that's how it has to be done. I promised Theo that I'd take Mom to court if she doesn't pay, and I will.

Mallory's Funeral Home sits on the corner of a busy intersection near Baptist-Haywood East. It's a beige brick structure with small stained glass windows on the long side. The short side includes the entrance hall and offices. They have two visitation rooms that can be made into four smaller rooms by sliding a partition across. I warn them that I don't expect to need more than a closet to hold the visitors, but they don't have anything smaller. They tell me about the men they will use as pallbearers – fifty dollars each to six students from the seminary. They'll attend the actual service and make the trip to Harmon. It's ten dollars an hour for each kid if we go beyond two hours. This is all 'normal' they tell me.

They warn me to expect only a trickle of visitors since most will come to the service at two. If we have five visitors I'll be surprised. I hope Brenda contacts Bobby and David, just for Dad's sake. I could almost come up with the pallbearers if

I could count on her boys, mine, Theo and Darnell. But relying on Bubbles is too risky.

The visitation room has two love seats flanked by end tables in each corner facing the hardwood area in front that holds the casket. The remainder of the seating is cushioned stackable chairs that line three walls. The room is carpeted and thick drapery cascades down behind the display area. Even now they are playing a soft classical piece in the background. I've decided to have that on during visitation. According to them it helps 'fill' the space.

The chapel is long with pews on both sides of a center aisle and smaller aisles against the walls. I'm told that it holds nearly two hundred people. Just a guess, but I think that's adequate. They recommend that we dispense with any 'family' type seating arrangement for the service. This will allow them to move everyone forward and avoid an unbalanced look. That sounds reasonable and should cover the first two or three rows.

I have one last thought, and I go back to the visitation room. Like the chapel, it has a large area where flowers are displayed around the casket. I've already counted the likely number of flower arrangements. I've ordered two big arrangements and the rose splay that sits atop the casket. Despite Mom's optimism and stingy habits, I'm worried that Dad will look bare. I tell them to go ahead and add the 'Basic Flower Additions' package number four. She can afford it.

The Reverend Dr. Reggie Halpern has been scheduled, and they assure me that he is experienced and does a nice job.

I think we're all set, and I go back home.

When Theo gets in, we have some wine, the good stuff, and I fix dinner. It's so nice to keep reminding myself that Brenda can argue with Mom about what to wear and every other little thing that Mom wants to argue about. Since she's in no position to take a contrary stand, there's no telling what craziness could transpire. I almost laugh about it to myself, but I try to remember the occasion.

#

It's Friday morning and I haven't shed a single tear. I've spent the last three months telling myself that they passed away thirty years ago, and it must be working.

Theo and I arrive a little before nine and T2, Ali and Brian are already here, sitting in the entrance hall. I didn't see anyone outside, nor did I recognize a car that one of us doesn't own. I guess Mom and Brenda will get here when they want to.

They lead us in, and all five of us go up to Dad's casket. He looks as reposed as he did at the hospital. We stand there in silence then talk about how good he looks. The kids give Theo and me a hug and move away. We stand there silently and I say another little prayer. He looks well groomed in his blue suit. It reminds me of back when we went to church.

I can hear a muffled exchange behind me, and when I turn I see T2 talking with one of the employees. He signals and I go over to them. They want to know if we want to hold the room private until Mrs. Ray has a chance to see him with his family? It's five after nine. I tell them to open it up at quarter after.

But we don't even wait that long. Some of Theo's school friends are already in the hallway. They're kind enough to come by, but they've got to get to work. I'm surprised to see some of them whom I haven't seen since last Christmas. So we're standing around talking about Dad and where he worked and where he grew up and the regular funeral parlor talk. Eventually they ask about Mom, and I have to say that she's coming with Brenda and that they should be here. Then I say I hope they didn't have a wreck, but I know they didn't. It's hard to say which one is responsible for failing to meet such a simple opening.

It's nearly nine-thirty, and I know the university people are hanging around to pay their respects to Mom. I don't even feel embarrassed — like it's some other family we're all waiting on. I walk out front and see a silver Kia. I watch as Brenda helps Mom get out of their new car. Mom's wearing a gray pants suit and Brenda's in her lavender one, probably the only one she has. But they look fine.

Everyone nods and smiles as they come through. I get on the other side of Mom and we go up to see Dad. She likes the suit I chose, it reminds her of Antioch where they went for thirty years. We stand here for several minutes and then back away. I point to one of the corners and ask her if she wants to sit there. She nods and we get her situated on the loveseat. Brenda sits down beside her, and one by one I introduce the people from school. They offer her their condolences, have a few last words with Theo who's joking about the department being off today and admonishing them to rescue the students from the graduate assistants. And they are all gone by ten. Now it's just my family, Brenda and Mom.

I'm not even going to ask them why they were late because I don't care. Brenda tells us anyway.

"We couldn't get her door locked," and she's laughing like it was a big adventure, but Mom's not smiling. "I couldn't figure it out; the key was stuck in there. We had to call them and wait for some guy to come over, and he just turns the key the right way, I guess, and it comes out."

"I kept telling you," says Mom. "Can't even lock a door," she mumbles almost under her breath. Then she looks toward the front. "Plenty of flowers. Sissy, do you know who they're all from?"

I do a Vanna White routine, standing at the front and reading the cards loudly, since we're the only ones in here. I had under-counted before, by three. One was from school, one is from T2's office, and one is from the Cancer Society. T2 and Ali have sent a beautiful huge arrangement, and Brian has one of similar design, but different colored flowers.

T2's bought all of them, and he's kidding Brian about working off what he owes by washing T2's fleet. Brian's laughing and saying he never agreed to buy a florist shop, he just wanted some flowers. I know Ali did it all because she's heard me talk about their paucity of friends.

"Who are the rest of them from?" Mom wants to know. I walk back over to her and tell her they are part of the package. I wait to see if she's got some greedy remark, but she's wise enough to keep her mouth shut.

"Darnell's coming by for the service," says Brenda and it makes me remember Carolyn. I know she'll be here sometime, and I wonder if she and Darnell will coordinate their visitation. I doubt it; they don't seem to be on great terms either. I have every intention of telling Carolyn exactly what I've told my family, which is the truth. I'll probably wait until another occasion, but I'll tell her. It's nothing against her brother, and I'm sure he won't miss me, but she deserves to know why I have disassociated myself from Mom and Brenda.

We stand around for the next hour, but not a soul comes through. Then, around lunch, some women from the cancer organization come by, as do some of our kid's friends. I knew it would be like this. Some other people from the university also come by, and I watch T2 do his networking thing. He's good, and they're all into computers so they have something in common.

By twelve-thirty the place is empty again. Ali comes in and tells us that there are refreshments in a small family room down the hall, if anybody wants some. Brenda has just returned from cigarette break number ten, and she asks Mom if she'd like some coffee or something. They follow

Ali down the hall. So now it's just Theo, T2, Brian and me. They're still in shock over the will, but they're doing a good job of hiding it.

We're all laughing about the lies I told, except T2 thinks the place in Florida is a good idea. He and Ali are excited about it. He's trying to talk Theo into finding a condo. "Prices are falling like a rock down there," he says. "It's the right time. A family place where we could all vacation. It'd be great," and he's talking about the locations.

Brenda comes back in a little before one. Mom's not feeling too well, and she's going to stay back there a little longer. Brenda's cell rings, and she hustles out of the room to take the call. When she comes back, she tells us that Darnell is coming. Great — I can't wait to meet him.

At a quarter past one Carolyn comes in. She tells us that Darnell is bringing their mom. Some of their family is coming by for the service at two. Ali's parents come in as well, so that's nice of them. They're both tall and lean, like Ali, and her mom is very pretty as well. Then Ali's brother and his wife come in, and I do a quick count in my head. If everything holds we'll have around fifteen people here for the service. I know that Ali has imposed on her family to make the service because she knows I'm concerned about an empty chapel.

Some more university people show up including Theo's whole office, so that's nice of them too. Hell, we may end up with twenty-five people in there. Then T2's office people come in — five of them. So the visitation room is starting to look more or less normal. I decide I better go and check on Mom.

"Where's Brenda?" I ask her.

"She's gone to meet him, Darnell what's his name." I want to say Davis-Ray so bad I can taste it, but I don't. I'm done with them so they can work it out later. I use it as a measure of my sanity that I can keep this stupid secret.

I explain that we have quite a few people in there and that I think she should come back in for a while before the service starts.

She grumbles about meeting all those people already and it's a big lie she's telling herself, like the place was packed all morning. "I'll be in there in a minute," she tells me.

When I get back I'm slightly, no, that's not right, I'm completely, totally shocked. The room is full of people and half of them are black.

Carolyn comes over and holds my elbow as she takes me over to her mom. Miss Sadie, as they call her, is a weathered old black woman with granny glasses and bright gray hair. She's wearing a black dress and a small tiara-type veil. Brenda is standing right beside her.

"Oh, Sissy," says Brenda, "I want you to meet Darnell," and she puts her hand on the giant black man standing beside her. He's nearly Theo's height but he must outweigh him by a hundred pounds. He's wearing a beautiful blue pin-stripe suit, modern, with three buttons all buttoned up. His blue tie has military symbols on it, and his white shirt is almost brilliant.

"How do you do?" he says. "I've heard about you," and he laughs.

"Thank you so much for coming," I tell him and his mom. "It's so nice to have you. To tell you the truth, I've been worried that we wouldn't have anyone here. My parents don't really have a bunch of friends. I look around. "Who are all these people?" I'm still shocked that he's black and shocked that all these black people are here. Shocked and incredibly delighted — absolutely joyous! I cannot wait until Mom comes in here. She is going to croak. I mean totally drop dead!

So Darnell begins the introductions with Carolyn's help. I can't possibly keep up with all the names. Theo is shaking hands and introducing Brian and T2 and Ali and it's like a giant reunion.

One of Darnell's ex-wives is here. She's bigger than Brenda, and I almost laugh thinking about what Carolyn said at T2's dinner. I position myself so I can see when Mom comes in. I don't give Brenda the satisfaction of even a short glimpse because I'm so busy meeting her new family. I wonder if she had any idea that they would be here in such numbers? I don't think she meant for it to happen like this.

Then Mom comes through the door. She's lucky that the room is buzzing with conversations. We're talking to a young man who goes to the university. Theo is telling him something about school. Theo's asking him questions, and the young man is smiling politely.

The whole time, I'm watching Mom. She comes to a full stop. She's looking around like she's in the wrong place. She shuffles back out to the hall, but she sees us and comes back in. To hell with her. I'm not going to introduce her new family, that's Brenda's job. But I'm sure going to be close enough to see her reaction. Talk about priceless.

Mom walks over to the loveseat and sits down. I'm waiting on Brenda, but she's trying to keep a low profile. For all I know she's not going to introduce them. I guess Mom can just assume that Dad had a bunch of black friends she didn't know about. She can do what she wants, but I'm obligated to introduce Carolyn and I'm not going to leave Ms. Sadie hanging out on a chair.

"Miss Sadie," I say, "would you and Carolyn like to meet my mother?" and Carolyn helps her up. Mom's got a look on her face that's a combination of shock and perplexity. She won't be perplexed for long.

"Mom, this is Carolyn Mullins. She works at a bank and she knows T2 from there. I told you I met her at his house. And this is her mother, Miss Sadie."

Carolyn sticks out her hand, and Mom shakes it. Ms. Sadie is saying that Dad looks younger than she expected, and Mom is sitting there with her mouth so open an elephant could fall in. Then Miss Sadie bends down and gives Mom a little kiss on her cheek. "I know how it is to lose a man," says Miss Sadie, "I've lost two — Carolyn's dad, about twenty years ago, and Donny, Darnell's dad, about two years ago. So I know what you're going through."

No you don't. You don't have any idea. But I do, and once again I'm having the devilish thought that there is a God, and he's a real practical joker. Mom's saying nothing. Her mouth is still open and her eyes are saying FIRE! Fire in here. And finally here comes Brenda with her husband, Darnell. Big Darnell. Big black Darnell. And following behind them is big black Darnell's extended family; his ex — his kids — his cousins.

"Mom," says Brenda, "I want you to meet Darnell. Darnell, this is my mother."

"How do you do Mrs. Ray? We're so sorry for your loss," and he looks at Miss Sadie. "Mom, why don't you sit with Mrs. Ray? Take a load off," and he helps her to sit down beside Mom. This is better than good – better than wonderful. I think for a second that I shouldn't feel this way at my father's funeral, but I quickly push that thought aside. Brenda has married an enormous black man and Mom's "never touched one in her life."

She has now.

Darnell reaches out his hand. "I'm sorry Mrs. Ray," he says again. "I wish I could have met him, but I've been working a lot lately." His hand is still sticking out there waiting on Mom, but she's in a state of shock and I'm not even sure she sees it.

"Mom," says Brenda. "You okay?"

She looks at Brenda. "Okay? Yes, yes," and slowly, ever so slowly, shaking and limp, her withered old hand sneaks out to meet Darnell's massive paw. He takes it in both hands and gives it a good squeeze.

"Now," says Darnell, "I want you to meet my family. We'll be the black sheep side," and he smiles.

"You're welcomed in this family," I say, but I don't look down at Mom. "Go ahead, please, introduce them."

"All right," says Darnell, and he wraps his hands together.

One by one they parade up to her and some shake and a couple bend to give her a short shallow hug, but nearly everyone touches her. I can tell that she's still in total shock. Even Brenda probably doesn't know about Mom's bigotry and racism, just me and Theo. And Mom.

She's gotten to where she'll nod a little bit, but she hasn't said a word. Ms. Sadie asks Carolyn to take her to the restroom before the service begins. She asks Mom if she needs to go, but Mom declines with a shake of her head. "Oh, no," she finally mumbles to the air.

I have to be careful because I'm in such a good mood. If I feel sorry for anyone, it's Darnell's family. He's the one that's traded down. What the hell was he thinking? As I look at his well-dressed family, I see all shades of people. I can't wait for Thanksgiving. I'm sure they have their own plans, but I'm going to invite them. Then I remember that I'm through with Brenda too, so that won't work. What a shame.

The lights flicker down and up. It's the signal to head into the chapel.

"C'mon, we'll help you," says Darnell as he and Brenda go to either side of Mom, and we all head down the hall to the chapel.

Theo better quit looking at me and making faces. I think he's deliberately trying to make me burst out laughing. Asshole.

Chapter 27: Status Change

The Bereavement Men are waiting for us at the entrance to the chapel. They're dressed identically in black suits, white shirts and black ties. "Mrs. Ray?" says one of them.

"This is my mom," I say and she takes a step forward.

"Okay," he says in that soft gentle funeral voice. "What we'd like to do is seat Mrs. Ray and the children on the first row. Who are the spouses," and he looks around.

"This is Theo," I say quickly and he shakes Theo's hand. I turn and look at Brenda.

"And this is Darnell," she says softly. He shakes Darnell's hand and Mom turns quickly to look at Brenda.

"What?" says Mom. "Is he a spouse?" she asks loudly.

Brenda has her hands locked in front of her. She smiles and nods. Then she grabs Darnell's arm and holds like a kid.

"Now, do we have any grandchildren?" says the man in black.

T2 and Brian holdup their hands.

"And us," and I look back and there's Bobby and David. I'm so happy to see them. I wish they'd have gotten here earlier. Then I see Billy back behind them. My God he looks like he's seventy five years old. Bobby and David move up with us. I give both of them a big hug, as does Theo. They shake hands with T2 and Brian, kids they played with for fifteen years at Mom and Dad's house.

The black suits can see that we're having a little reunion so they just wait. Bobby and David come up and give Mom a hug, and I know that she would normally be so glad to see them, but events have overtaken her and she just looks forward into the chapel.

"Okay," says the head bereavement man, and he looks at the grandkids, "We'll put all four of you on the right front. There's room for maybe two spouses," and he waits expectantly.

"Do you have wives?" I ask Bobby and David. They both shake their heads. "Okay," I tell him, "it's just her," and I point to Ali.

He looks up. "The rest of you just fill in on either side. Doesn't matter. We'll try to get everyone up to the front." He turns back to Mom. "Mrs. Ray," he says and he sticks out his elbow. She's in a daze as she puts her hand on his arm. We watch them head down the aisle. Theo and I go next. They sit Mom in the middle of the left pew. I sit to her left and Theo sits to my left. Then Brenda and Darnell come down. Brenda sits to her right and Darnell sits to Brenda's right, on the center aisle.

The four grandkids and Ali come down next and they all take the other front row. Then everybody else follows in.

But it just keeps getting better. Up on the platform sits the casket and flowers on the right and a chair holding what I imagine to be Reverend Halpern on the left, right in front of Mom. He's short, fat, and black. It's perfect. I couldn't have planned it better if I had thought of it myself.

The music is playing softly and eventually
everyone gets seated, but we are too somber to turn
and look behind us. I can see that Mom's mouth is
still open and her face looks frozen into a
permanent state of shock. Good for her. It occurs
to me that once they change that will, if Mom and
Brenda were to die, I guess Darnell would get the
money? Wow. You talk about God kicking her in
the teeth. That would be better than even me
getting it. Mom's money going to Darnell. She'd
roll over in her grave for sure.

We're all sitting quietly listening to the music
and waiting for the Reverend to start. I'm not sure
if he's praying or sleeping, but his eyes are closed.
Good news, I see him peek out at the assembled.
He's in no hurry.

I'm sitting here thinking about how
completely stupid and greedy Brenda is. I don't
think she ever intended for Mom to know about
Darnell. The business with the will was concocted
before Dad got sick. She had already told me she
didn't even know if she was going to tell Mom.
Well, I know, and she wasn't. But she can't hide
him here.

But why did she tell me about him? She
knows I could have told Mom at any time. It's like
a lot of things with her –confused and inconsistent.
A thorough review of Brenda's actions would show
random acts of personal satisfaction layered over
selfishness with a touch of opportunism thrown in
willy-nilly. The available evidence would indicate
no pattern whatsoever. Any conclusion that
attributed planning and conspiring to Brenda would

give her credit for doing something completely foreign to her nature.

A more charitable explanation is that she put off doing what she should have done – simple procrastination. She probably didn't think about how Mom would view Darnell and his family. I didn't know about Mom's late life transformation into a bigoted racist until very recently. Maybe it wasn't a transformation? Maybe it was always there, but never had an opportunity to present itself? Maybe it's like a virus that lies dormant for years, eighty-plus in her case, before being activated by environmental circumstances?

Or maybe Mom had better sense and kept it hidden. "I ain't touched one in my life and I ain't starting now," that's what she said. Careful about prognostications, they can come back to bite you, or touch you in this case.

We weren't raised that way. We never heard a disparaging comment about black people, or any other people for that matter. I don't think it ever came up, at least not that I can recall. I have to thank Mom and Dad for that. So whatever animosity she had went un-expressed. Brenda certainly wasn't infected— Darnell's proof of that. I want to be reasonable and charitable sitting in this chapel with Dad and all these people. The whole business with the will is uncomfortable, enlightening and liberating.

The rotund Reverend stands up, and the music trails off. He walks to the podium and opens the Bible. He stands there looking out over the room. He could use Darnell's tailor. He smiles hugely, an infectious smile that makes me feel better.

"Welcome to the House of the Lord," he says. "Mrs. Ray, Ms. Sissy and Ms. Brenda, we join with you today to celebrate the life of Stanley Ray, a good man by all accounts. We welcome all of his family and friends.

"My, my," he says looking at all of us. "Mr. Ray, Stanley, would surely be pleased to see a group such as this. A group so obviously free of the turmoil which seems at times to overtake us, and overwhelm us. The group I see here today is the picture of what Dr. King had in mind so many years ago. It's a picture he died for. But it's also a picture that comes to us courtesy of Mr. Stanley Ray. It says more about him than I will ever be able to put into words. God bless him for that."

There is a chorus of low, muffled amen's from the new side of my family – from Brenda's family.

"Let us bow our heads now as I read from . . ." and as I bow my head, I notice that Mom has finally moved. She's closed her eyes and she rests her chin on her chest. I wonder what she's thinking about his opening lines. I know that the Reverend has misinterpreted the diverse attendance at this occasion. But I give him credit for giving Dad credit, even if it is only indirectly deserved. I hope that Mom is reviewing her prejudices as he prays. Perhaps she's having a cathartic transformation back to being a decent human being. Perhaps this 'untouchable' has managed to touch her in some way.

The Reverend Halpern talks at length about the 'good man.' He has a beautiful sing-song melody that is soothing and comforting, even if I've paid little attention to every word.

"And finally," he says, "for you Mrs. Ray, for Ms. Sissy and Ms. Brenda, and for all of his friends and wonderful family gathered here, I read the words of our Lord to his disciples in their hours of confusion. From John, Chapter Sixteen, Verse Twenty: 'Verily, verily, I say unto you, that you shall weep and lament, but the world shall rejoice: And you shall be sorrowful, but your sorrow shall be turned into joy.'"

The mention of my name makes me pay attention. He waits and then closes his book. He closes his eyes and bows his head. "Dear God, dear Jesus, accept into your loving arms the soul of Stanley Ray. Hold him tight and give us the strength to recognize that his passing is a temporary loss. Help us to recognize that we will join him soon. Comfort Mrs. Ray with the sure knowledge that he remains close to her, waiting for her in the eternal light of our Lord. Amen."

There's another chorus of amen's. The Reverend Halpern steps down and places the bible on Mom's lap. She is still bowed in prayer, or asleep, I'm not sure which. He takes her wrist, and places her hand on the Bible. I see him jerk, slightly. He steps back and his eyes are wide. He looks up at us and says, "If everyone will wait in the visitation room, the immediate family will join you there. Thank you for coming," and he almost pushes them out. "Yeah," he says, "go on now," and he's standing with his hand on Darnell's shoulder to hold him in place. Bobby starts to get up, but the Reverend moves to him quickly and places his hand on Bobby's shoulder and pushes him back down. He wants everyone out of the chapel except the first row.

"Wait here," he says and he goes to the back of the room. He has a conversation with one of the Bereavement Boys. I turn and see the man hustle off while the Reverend pulls the doors shut behind him. It all seems unusual. I'm wondering if he wants to say something to us. I look at Mom, and she hasn't moved for five minutes. It seems like she's clutching that Bible. I give her a slight poke to let her know that he wants to talk with us. She doesn't move. I scoot away a few inches and grab her arm. I shake it a bit and her hand falls off the Bible and slaps the pew.

Brenda's bent down looking up into her face. "Mom!" she says loudly. "Mom!" and she gives her a good shake and Mom's head rolls around.

"I'm sorry," says Reverend Halpern. "Please, I think your mother is, is passed. I've told the director. He has an emergency vehicle coming.

We all stand up, and Ali lets out a cry. "You mean she's dead?" she says, and she's covering her mouth like it was a mistake to acknowledge the possibility. But I know she is. She's died during the ceremony. We're all standing and Theo has me all wrapped up in his arms. He helps me to sit on the pew. I can feel myself breathing deeply, trying to catch my breath. My head feels light and I need to lie down, but I know this isn't the time to sleep.

It's not the right thing to do. This is the time when I have to be strong. I raise my head. Brenda is standing beside me. She caresses my head and holds it against her. I can feel her sobbing.

I think about Mom's soul. Where is it? Who wants that soul? Can it be repaired? Is it worth repairing? I commend her soul to God's judgment. Thank God, He'll have to decide. I look up at Theo. I give him my hand and he helps me to stand.

"I'm so sorry," says Reverend Halpern. "I've never had this happen before. I'm so sorry for your loss," and he's standing there like he doesn't know what to do, and he probably doesn't.

T2 walks over. "We have to tell them," he says. "I'll go. Mom, you and Dad, let's see what we can arrange now. Wait here," and he heads down the aisle just as the doors open up. It's one of the men in black. T2 puts his arm around the man's shoulder and together they go back out to the front as the doors slowly close.

"Thank you Reverend," says Theo. "It was a wonderful homily. We'll be in touch," and he dismisses the good Reverend. He hugs each of us as he leaves. "God bless you," he says, and then he heads down the aisle. He seems stricken. I stand up and catch him at the back.

He turns, and we hug. "This is what God wanted," I tell him because I don't know what else to say. I just want to let him know that he has nothing to do with this. This is God's doing. Maybe it's His way of delivering poetic justice, I don't know, but it's got nothing to do with Reverend Halpern. It's really between me and

Mom, that's all—just us two. It's not really between her and Brenda.

He leaves, and I walk back to the front. "I just wanted to let him know that he didn't bore her to death," I say, and I laugh a little short, sober laugh. But it's enough to relieve the tension. I don't even worry what the others will think. I'm beyond that. I have a new strength that overcomes my inclination to cry. Mom can have all the credit for that. Mom has prepared me for this mini-crucible. Sissy's lament is so short that it's already come and gone.

#

T2 is the model of efficiency. He stands in front of all of us in the visitation room. Mom's funeral will be tomorrow. We'll take them together to Harmon. Please don't send more flowers. Check the obituary for any changes, but for right now it will be from ten till two, service, and then burial. He thanks everyone for coming and hopes they can make it tomorrow, but the family will understand if other plans interfere. Perhaps you can get by in the morning, he says. Reverend Halpern will return. He requested it, says T2.

This is like work, an untimely death has let us off early, and tomorrow we'll be on overtime.

Chapter 28: My New Family

Mom's funeral has more of a family reunion feel than Dad's. I guess we all know each other. The Reverend Halpern is now Reverend Reggie, and he and Darnell are talking like they've known each other for years.

It's almost the same group of people. T2 told us last night that when he told everyone about Mom the only one who said anything was Miss Sadie. "Well, I'll be damned," she said.

She repeated that sentiment today, adding, "I never seen someone so eager to join their husband. He must have been a damn sight better than those fellers I married." She's funny without even trying.

The Reverend's homily was very touching and personal, but it couldn't have been less accurate. She was only a few of the nice things he said about her, and even they were a stretch.

Theo paid the pallbearers yesterday, and we had plenty for today; David, Bobby, T2, Brian, Tayshaun, and Juan. They had to do double duty, but to Mallory's credit, everything went fine and proper decorum was maintained.

Seven cars, two hearses, and two limos made the trip to Harmon. It's not as far as I remember. The plots are on a gentle hillside, and the cemetery is picturesque. It's the right place, even though we discussed the possibility of moving them in closer. But this is where they wanted to be, even if Mom's reasons are, well, suspect.

We've passed by my palm tree Oasis twice. Someone was parked in my spot both times.

#

We're at T2's now, along with our new
family. It must be nice to have money. T2 has an
impromptu gathering catered and there is even a
bartender. A lot of those folks who couldn't make
it out to Harmon have better luck making it to their
new rich relative's house. Carolyn can be
congratulated for spreading the word about the
mansion long before any of this. Ali is simply the
best hostess I've ever seen – gracious and
accommodating, she flits around making sure
everyone is included.

Theo and I have had a few moments alone
together as we drive to T2's. He agrees that I need
to put this will business to bed. I catch Brenda
returning from the restroom.

"You got a minute," I ask her.

"Oh sure," and I can see the trepidation on
her face. She has every right to be worried. Unless
I misunderstand things, I'm in charge of the estate.

She follows me into T2's office. It's all
beautiful wood with hi-tech stuff built into desks
and walls. She sits on a leather sofa and I take a
matching wingback chair.

"I want to talk with you about the will," I say.

"Oh," and she starts to wipe her eyes.

"Wait a minute," I say. "Just hold on. I want
to forget about everything else."

"I'm so sorry," she says, and she probably is.
I don't want her to say anything, really. I don't
want her to ruin a case that she doesn't need to
make.

"Look, I'm not sure about all the legal things that have to happen. I just want you to know that their estate will be divided up between the two of us. That's how it's supposed to be and that's how I want it. So I'll look into it next week and tell you what I find out. The only things I want from the house are the pictures and my old bedroom suit. You can have the rest. Okay?"

She nods, and I think she finally gets it because she doesn't say anything. That's the first smart thing she's done in years, unless I count Darnell, and the jury is still out on that partnership.

I suppose I take it as a measure of my mental well-being that I'm willing to be so magnanimous. Brenda certainly didn't earn it, but, at the same time, I have to feel that Mom has perverted nearly everything she's touched. I've also thought about my Grandma. I don't know if there's a genetic link that explains things, but I don't intend for it to survive into future generations.

I stand up. "Okay. That's the way it will be."

"I love you," she says. She stands, and I give her a hug.

"We better get out of here," and we return to the family.

Epilogue: An Ode to the Palm Trees

We need to have this boat back to port by the twentieth. They require a day to clean and provision her for the next group who intend to spend Christmas on it. But that still gives us another six days.

Sheldon and Theo are comparing their new handheld GPS's to the one mounted in the lower helm. They finally agree that they know exactly where we are on planet earth. This is reassuring to me, but Deidra never doubted them. She wants Sheldon to speed it up, to hell with the fuel burn. She keeps praying that the next cove is empty, but at the same time she admits that it is a popular place and it's first come, first anchored.

By now Theo and Sheldon understand the graphical interface and the GPS overlay. They keep saying things like, marker, and waypoint. "That's her," says Sheldon and he points ahead.

"We'll know soon enough," says Deidra. Sheldon slows the boat and looks at all the electronics, but he also steps out of the pilothouse door to look at the water in front and below. Theo is on the pulpit watching carefully for any unwanted discoloration that might indicate shallow water.

Deidra lets out a cheer as we round a sandy point. "Empty as shit." she screams. "It's ours now. Ours!"

I can see why she is so excited. The spot is beautiful. We drop anchor right in the middle, back way off, throw a second anchor off the back, pull forward, and shut down.

We're in a beautiful cerulean bowl surrounded by beaches. With the tide up, there's only thirty or forty feet from water to the palm tree line. It takes us fifteen minutes to lower the whaler with the davit thing that has a habit of shorting out.

We have everything ready. We load the tender and head to the beach. Everywhere I look my palm trees are exact duplicates of these. They're reassuring to me.

Deidra and Sheldon gather up some stuff and head off. They intend to go nude sunbathing around the point of this tiny island. Maybe it's our age, or Sheldon's portly figure, but it strikes me as funny. But I don't say anything except goodbye as they shuffle off.

Ten minutes later Theo and I are nude. For some reason, what seemed crazy seems sensible. I guess that's just how life is, and there's really nothing lamentable about it. I don't want to be overly optimistic, but it doesn't get any better than this.

The End

Made in the USA
Middletown, DE
05 July 2016